Khuc Cay

Adorable Amigurumi Christmas

10 sweet crochet projects to make and treasure

SEARCH PRESS

First published in the UK in 2026 by
Search Press Limited
Wellwood, North Farm Road,
Tunbridge Wells, Kent TN2 3DR

1 2 3 4 5 6 7 8 9 10

Original French title: *Le Noël de Khuc Cay*

Editorial photographs: Fabrice Besse and Sonia Roy
Step-by-step photographs and sketches of designs: Khuc Cay

English translation by Tankerton Translations.

ISBN: 978-1-80092-416-1
eBook ISBN: 978-1-80093-374-3

Bookmarked Hub
For further ideas and inspiration, and to join our free online community, visit www.bookmarkedhub.com

Publishers' notes
Metric measurements are used in this book; the imperial conversions are rounded to the nearest ¼in. Always use either metric or imperial measurements, not a combination of both.

UK crochet terms are used throughout this book. For a UK to US conversion chart please refer to page 24 and the inside front flap.

For errata, please visit our website (www.searchpress.com) or the Bookmarked Hub (www.bookmarkedhub.com).

You are invited to visit the author's
Website: www.khuccay.com
Instagram: @lespetitesmainsdekhuccay
Facebook: KHUC CAY

GPSR information can be found at www.searchpress.com
Printed in China, RRD032026.

BEFORE YOU BEGIN

- The materials and techniques used to make the toys in this book are described in more detail on pages 10 to 25.
- If you come up against any problems as you are working, do not hesitate to refer back to these pages to find the solution. You can also check out my YouTube channel (@KhucCay) where you will find videos explaining some of the techniques and various crocheting tips.
- If, despite this, you need more detailed instructions, do not hesitate to contact me, I will be happy to help.

Introduction

I was born and grew up in Vietnam in the early 1990s. At this time, Christmas was a distant, exotic, fascinating festivity for me. We had heard about it from friends who lived in a neighbouring Christian village, and I remember being very intrigued when they told us how much fun they had during this strange holiday.

For my secondary education, I moved to a school in the centre of the city of Hanoi. A few days before Christmas, a handful of students would go from room to room, selling pretty little cards. This was the first time I learnt that Christmas was also a time for sending cards, even for non-Christians. In the years that followed, Christmas was a great opportunity to get together with friends and wander through the light-filled streets of Hanoi. We would wish each other all the best, a bit like at New Year.

However, I did not experience my first real Christmas until I arrived in France and got married. During the cold December days, my mother-in-law would be busy decorating the house and bringing out the dusty old boxes full of tinsel, baubles and tree decorations. We would put up pine branches in the windows, deck the house with fairy lights and decorate the Christmas tree. I was as excited as a child! We even went to the Alsace region to experience the incredible atmosphere of the famous Christmas markets.

After the birth of my daughter, Anna, Christmas seemed even more magical to me. The legend of Santa Claus, his elves and the flying reindeer brought a sense of wonder to the whole family. We all began to believe in the fabulous characters and magical stories we read together every evening.

For me, this book is an opportunity to invite you into our wonderful world. As you turn the pages, you will meet Leon the polar bear who delivers children's letters to Santa Claus, the charming elves in charge of getting the toys ready, a train full of presents driven by Alex the gingerbread man, and even my daughter Anna who, like so many other children, is always impatient to open her presents.

You will also find inside detailed techniques, along with tips to help you make your new favourite soft toys. I hope you will feel inspired to be creative and add your own special touches to your characters.

I would love this book to sprinkle the magic of Christmas over you, and I am certain that you will make some splendid decorations to make the festivities even more special.

Happy crocheting to one and all!

Khuc Cay (Hoang Thi Ngoc Anh)

Contents

THE DESIGNS

What you need

THE YARN

CROCHET YARN

There is a huge variety of yarn that you can use to make toys – choose the one that you prefer. It is essential, however, that there is no elasticity in the yarn. This will ensure that your work holds its shape during the stuffing stage. I recommend trying out different types of yarn to find the one that suits you best. Use the yarn weights and yardage given to substitute other brands, if you prefer.

For this book, I have worked with DMC yarns as listed:

- **DMC Natura Just Cotton** – 4-ply (fingering/weight 1) 100% cotton yarn; 50g/1¾oz/155m/170yd – allows you to work fine details;
- **DMC Happy Cotton** – DK (8-ply/light/worsted/weight 3), 100% cotton yarn; 20g/¾oz/43m/47yd – is the ideal thickness for crocheting amigurumis. Thicker than Natura Just Cotton, it is very easy for beginners to use – note, however, that this range only comes in 43m/47yd balls, so you need to make sure you have enough;

- **DMC 100% Baby Cotton** – DK (8-ply/light worsted/weight 3), 100% cotton yarn; 50g/1¾oz/106m/116yd – this is similar to Happy Cotton; some colours are more or less identical, but the balls are bigger;
- **DMC Woolly yarn** – 5-ply (sport weight/ weight 2) 100% Merino wool; 50g/1¾oz/125m/137yd – this pure Merino wool, widely acknowledged as the best wool in the world, can be combined with Natura Just Cotton and Happy Cotton, using different sizes of crochet hook. It is well suited to making clothes for soft toys;
- **DMC Woolly Chic yarn** – 5-ply (sport weight/ weight 2) 96% Merino wool, 4% polyester; 50g/1¾oz/125m/137yd – this is a top-of-the-range yarn in Merino wool with a metallic glimmer. It will lend an original touch to your creations;
- **DMC Teddy yarn** – 5-ply (sport weight/ weight 2) 100% polyamide; 50g/1¾oz/90m/98yd – this yarn is voluminous and very soft to the touch, giving soft toys a special texture;
- **DMC Knitty 4 yarn** – DK (8-ply/light worsted/weight 3) 100% acrylic; 50g/1¾oz/140m/153yd – this is a thick yarn that is warm for winter;
- **Big Knit yarn** – Chunky (bulky/weight 5) 80% acrylic, 20% wool; 200g/7oz/106m/116yd: this is very soft and thick, perfect for making dolls' hair, using a fine felting needle (recognizable by the little notches along it), which you punch into the base several times to attach the yarn;
- **Velvet yarn** – Super chunky (super bulky/ weight 6) 100% polyester; 100g/3½oz/100m/109yd – this yarn is extremely soft to the touch, giving creations a bit of volume;
- **Lumina yarn** – 4-ply (fingering/weight 1), 60% viscose, 40% metallic polyester; 20g/¾oz/150m/164yd); this yarn is is metallic and shiny, which is useful for adding some little Christmassy touches.

Depending on the tension you apply and your crocheting style, you might need more or less yarn for your creations. All the same, I give the number of balls that I have used at the beginning of each pattern, which you can use as a guide. Remember that the types and colours of yarns that I use are just options; you can, of course, choose others according to your preferences in order to create really unique items.

EMBROIDERY THREAD

You will also need embroidery thread to embroider the noses and the eyes of your characters (if you are not using safety eyes – see page 8), and for other small decorative elements. The yarn you use for crocheting can also be used for embroidering the details. In this book, I have used DMC Coton Perlé in size 8, colours black (310) and brown (938).

HOOKS

It is important to work with high-quality hooks for the comfort of your fingers. Everyone has a different way of holding their hook, so you need to find the models that you find the most comfortable. I hold my hook like a pen (see right) and I find that the Clover Soft Touch hooks, which have a wide plastic handle, are the most comfortable to use. I have not used anything else since I first discovered them.

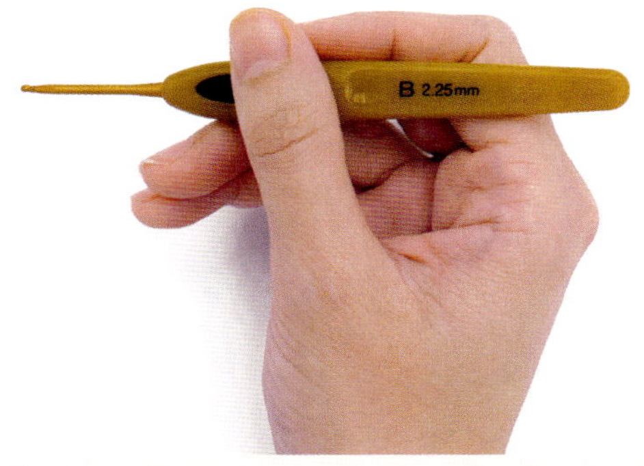

I advise opting for hooks one or two sizes smaller than the size recommended on the balls so that your stitches are tight and no holes appear when stuffing.

- I use a **2.25mm (UK 13, US 1) hook** with the Natura Just Cotton and Lumina yarns; a **2.5mm (UK 12/13, US 1/2) hook** with the Happy Cotton, 100% Baby Cotton, Teddy and Knitty yarns; and a **4mm (UK 8, US 6) hook** for the Velvet yarns.
- The Woolly and Woolly Chic yarns can be worked using **2.25mm (UK 13, US 1)** and **2.5mm (UK 12/13, US 1/2) hooks**, and when the design also includes Natura Just Cotton, I use the **2.25mm (UK 13, US 1) hook**. When it also includes Happy Cotton, I use the **2.5mm (UK 12/13, US 1/2)**.

Whatever the yarn, the size of hook to use is always given at the start of the pattern.

Counting stitches between the eyes.

SAFETY EYES

Several types of safety eyes are available on the market to give your soft toys a more expressive look. For each pattern, I specify the recommended size. It is important that they should be of a good quality to ensure they do not get lost or torn off. Safety eyes can be bought in craft shops and haberdashery departments, as well as online.

RECOMMENDATION

If the toy is for a child under the age of three, it is best to embroider the eyes rather than clip on plastic ones, even if they are classed as 'safety' eyes.

POMPOM MAKER

You will need to make a pompom for some of the designs. There are several ways of doing this, using a fork or cardboard rings, for instance. To simplify the process, I use a pompom maker that produces pompoms of different sizes, and follow the instructions that came with it.

BASIC KIT

YARN NEEDLE

Use a yarn needle to sew together the different parts of your soft toy. A steel needle is softer and easier to use than a plastic needle. I prefer the Clover curved needle, which I find very practical. Its pointed tip makes it easier to sew without exerting too much force, limiting the pain in your fingers.

STITCH MARKERS

Personally, I do not use stitch markers, as I have got into the habit of counting the stitches in my head. However, I would recommend them to you for marking the beginning or end of each round to help you keep track of your stitch count.

You can use a marker ring, a paper clip or a hair grip. The most important thing is to ensure the marker is carefully placed in the correct stitch, and to count the number of stitches for each round without making any errors. In this book in particular, they are many colour changes and counting your stitches is the key to success.

STUFFING

I use polyester wadding (batting) for my stuffing as it is easy to find at a low cost. Toy wadding can also be made from cotton or wool.

The stuffing stage is very important when you are making your creations. You must stuff fairly firmly to ensure an attractive result and that the soft toy holds its shape. Make sure not to over-stuff, otherwise you risk pushing the stitches apart, which will mean you can see the wadding (batting).

I would recommend adding stuffing as you go along and comparing the shape of the soft toy with the model in the photograph. For each part of each design, I tell you the stage at which you should start stuffing. If it is not given, it is because it is not necessary – for example for the arms.

BLUSHER AND A PAINTBRUSH

I like to add a little blusher to the cheeks of my soft toys with a paintbrush.

ROUND-HEADED PINS

These are very useful tools for marking the position of any elements that need to be embroidered or to hold different sections together before making up. Holding the pieces temporarily in place with these pins will allow you to adjust their position and check on symmetry before sewing together. You can also use the pins as markers for the centre of the face – this makes it much easier to ensure you are embroidering the details of your soft toy in the right places.

SCISSORS

A small pair of scissors is essential for cutting the yarn once you have finished making your piece.

OPTIONAL SUPPLIES

I sometimes add buttons, ribbons or different fabrics to my makes, for some touches of originality. I might also use wire to make spectacles. However, if you are making soft toys for children under the age of three, it is best to avoid using buttons or wire.

Crochet techniques

UK crochet terms are used throughout this book. For a UK to US conversion chart please refer to page 24.

STITCHES

CHAIN STITCH (ch)

1 Tie a slip knot on the hook (**1**).

2 Wrap the yarn over the hook (**2**) and draw the yarn through the first loop (**3**). Repeat as many times as required to make a foundation chain (**4**).

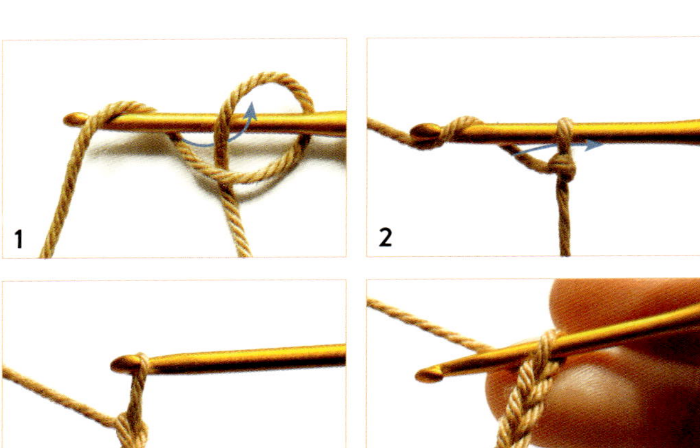

WHAT IS A 'YARN OVER'?

To work a yarn over, you simply need to wrap the yarn over the hook before or after having inserted the hook into a stitch. You can pass the yarn under or over the hook (see the X-shaped double crochet stitch on page 11, which illustrates the two versions of yarn over).

SLIP STITCH (sl st)

1 Insert the hook into the stitch (**1**).

2 Wrap the yarn over the hook (**2**) and draw the yarn through the first loop (**3**). Repeat as many times as required to make a foundation chain (**4**).

DOUBLE CROCHET (DC)

V-SHAPED DOUBLE CROCHET

This is the classic double crochet.

1 Insert the hook into the stitch (**1**).

2 Wrap the yarn over the hook and draw the yarn through the first loop on the hook (**2**).

3 Wrap the yarn over the hook again and draw the yarn through the two loops on the hook (**3 and 4**).

X-SHAPED DOUBLE CROCHET

If you work the two yarn overs that you need to form a double crochet stitch in the same way, namely over the hook, the stitch you obtain will be V-shaped. However, if you work the first yarn under the hook (**1**) and the second over (**2**), the stitch will be X-shaped. I think this gives a denser, more attractive finish.

To work X-shaped double crochet stitches, follow the steps below.

1 Insert the hook into the stitch, wrap the yarn under, passing it under the hook.

2 Draw the yarn through the first loop. Wrap the yarn over the hook and draw the yarn through the two loops.

V-shaped stitches (left) and X-shaped stitches (right) using the same hooks and yarn and following the same pattern.

HALF-TREBLE (htr)

1 Wrap the yarn over the hook and insert the hook into the stitch (**1**).
2 Wrap the yarn over the hook again and draw the yarn back through (**2**).
3 Wrap the yarn over the hook for the last time and draw the yarn through the three loops on the hook (**3 and 4**).

TREBLE (tr)

1 Wrap the yarn over the hook and insert the hook into the stitch (**1**).
2 Wrap the yarn over the hook again and draw the yarn back through (**2**).
3 Wrap the yarn over the hook for a third time and draw the yarn through the first two loops on the hook (**3**).
4 Wrap the yarn over the hook for a fourth and final time and draw the yarn through the two remaining loops on the hook (**4 and 5**).

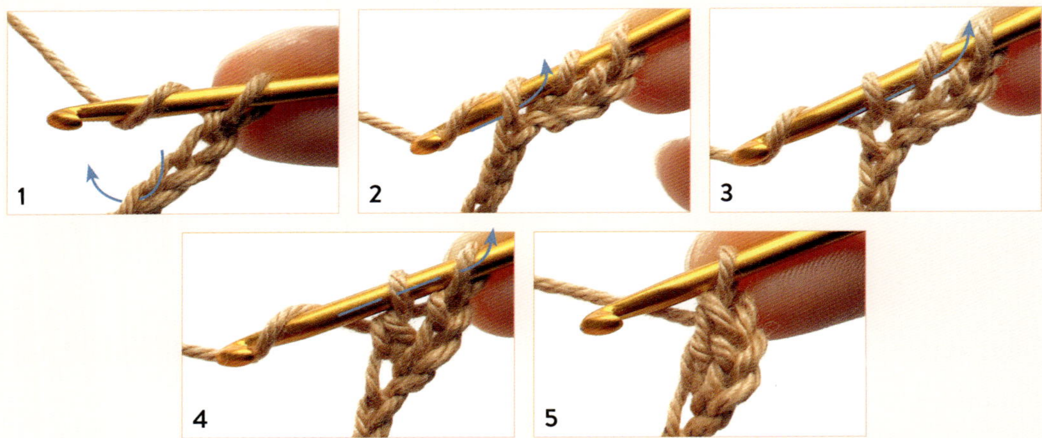

DOUBLE TREBLE (dtr)

1 Wrap the yarn over the hook twice and insert the hook into the stitch (**1**).
2 Wrap the yarn over the hook for a third time and draw the yarn back through (**2**).
3 Wrap the yarn over the hook for a fourth time and draw the yarn through the first two loops on the hook (**3**).
4 Wrap the yarn over the hook for a fifth time and draw the yarn through the first two loops on the hook (**4**).
5 Wrap the yarn over the hook for a sixth and final time and draw the yarn through the two remaining loops on the hook (**5 and 6**).

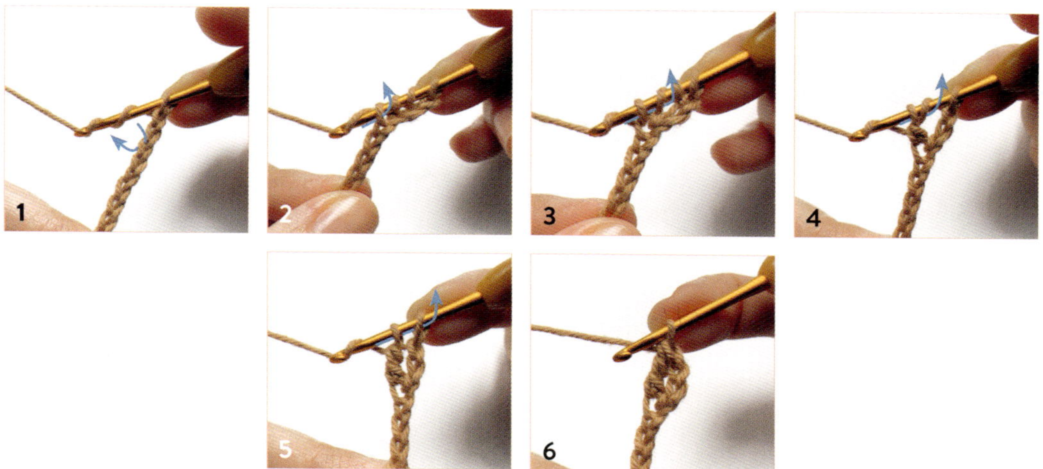

POPCORN STITCH (PC)

1 Wrap the yarn over the hook, insert the hook into the relevant stitch or space and draw through a loop (three loops on the hook), wrap the yarn over again and draw the yarn through the first two loops on the hook (two loops remain on the hook) (**1**).

2 Repeat *yarn over, insert hook in same place and draw through a loop, yarn over again and draw the yarn through the first two loops on the hook* three more times from * to *, until you have five loops on the hook (**2**).

3 Wrap the yarn over the hook for the last time and draw the yarn through the five loops on the hook (**3**).

INCREASE (inc)

Work two of the same stitches into a single stitch.

DECREASE (dec)

SIMPLE DOUBLE CROCHET DECREASE

1 Insert the hook into the stitch, yarn over hook and draw the yarn back through (two loops on the hook).

2 Insert the hook into the next stitch, yarn over hook, then draw the yarn back through (three loops on the hook).

3 Wrap the yarn over the hook and draw the yarn through the three loops.

INVISIBLE DECREASE

1 Insert the hook into the front loop of each of the next two stitches (**1**). Yarn over hook and draw the yarn back through (two loops on the hook) (**2**).
2 Wrap the yarn over the hook and draw the yarn through the two loops (**3**).

Use invisible decreases throughout when decreasing in double crochet.

NOTE

For a perfect result, I always use an invisible decrease.

1

2

3

GENERAL TECHNIQUES

MAKING AN ADJUSTABLE RING

This is the perfect way to start work in the round. It is ideal because it means you do not end up with the hole in the centre that you can get when the ring is made using a foundation chain.
1 Make a loop with the yarn. Pass the hook through this loop and draw the working yarn (the yarn leading to the ball) inside the loop as if to form a slip knot, but without pulling it tight (**1 and 2**).
2 Pinching the circle between your thumb and middle finger, wrap the working yarn round your forefinger as you would normally to hold the yarn straight. Wrap the yarn over the hook (**3**) then draw the yarn through the loop on the hook. This will secure the adjustable ring. This chain stitch does not count as a first stitch (**4**).
3 Work the number of double crochets indicated in the pattern as follows: insert the hook into the middle of the ring and wrap the yarn over. Draw the yarn through the circle (**5**), keeping the end of the yarn up against the ring, then wrap the yarn over again (**6**) and draw the yarn through the two loops on the hook. You have worked your first double crochet (**7**).
3 Pull firmly on the end of the yarn to close up the adjustable ring (**8 and 9**).

1

2

3

WORKING SPIRAL ROUNDS

If nothing is specified in the pattern, it is best to work in spiral rounds, without fastening off the rounds with a slip stitch. This makes the joins between the rounds of a spherical piece almost invisible, which is why you need to use a stitch marker to identify where the round you are currently working begins and ends. This technique is used for making round pieces. In this case, start with an adjustable ring (see page 14). At the end of the first round, attach a marker to the last stitch of the round. At the end of each round, remove the marker from the initial stitch, work it, and replace the ring in this latest stitch. You then begin the new round. Continue crocheting as normal until you get back to the marked stitch.

WORKING JOINED ROUNDS

Fasten off each round with a slip stitch into the first stitch of the previous round. The next round begins with a chain, worked with the number of chain stitches given in the pattern. These chain stitches do not count as a stitch. The first stitch of this round will be worked into the same stitch as this chain stitch.

NOTE

Do not turn your work over at the end of each round unless the pattern instructs you to do so.

WORKING AROUND A FOUNDATION CHAIN

After having made a foundation chain (**1**), work a double crochet into the second chain from the hook. Work double crochets along the chain until the end (**2**), then continue on the other side (**3 and 4**).

1

2

3

4

WORKING IN ROWS

Crochet a row (**1**). At the end of this row, turn your work and start the new row with a chain, worked with the number of chain stitches given in the pattern (**2**). Repeat until the piece is completed (**3**).

1

2

3

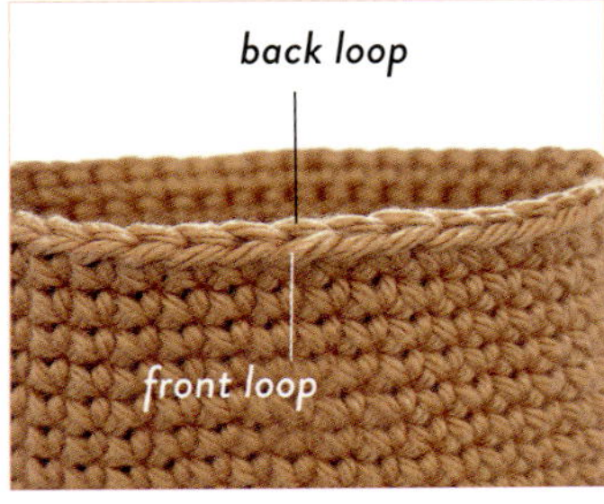

WORKING INTO THE FRONT AND BACK LOOPS

Stitches always have two loops:

- the front loop is the one closest to you;
- the back loop is the one furthest away.

To make some parts of a design, you will sometimes need to work into only one of these loops which will give you a raised texture.

DIFFERENTIATING THE INSIDE FROM THE OUTSIDE

It is important that the work is the right way out so it is the one intended to be the outside (the right side, **1**) that shows. The inside (wrong side, **2**) should be invisible on the inside. This will ensure the more attractive side is the one you can see.

1

2

ADAPTING THE FINAL SIZE

The final size of the toy will depend on several factors: yarn thickness, hook size, the tension you apply and what type of single crochet you use (X or V). The size of the soft toys is given at the start of each pattern, using the given list of findings and working in special double crochet (X-shaped). For bigger soft toys, use a thicker yarn and bigger hook, and the reverse for smaller toys.

These balls have been made following the same pattern, but I worked the one on the right with Happy Cotton yarn (DMC) and a 2.5mm (UK 12/13, US 1/2) hook; for the one on the left, I used Natura Just Cotton yarn (DMC) and a 2.25mm (UK 13, US 1) crochet hook.

CHANGING COLOUR OR YARN

Colour changes are always worked on the last stitch in colour 1.

1 Insert the hook into the last stitch in colour A. Wrap yarn A over and draw the yarn through the stitch, as if you were going to work a normal double crochet (two loops on the hook).

2 Set colour A to one side. Wrap colour B over the hook (**1**) and draw the yarn through the two loops (**2**). Pull on colour A to tighten the stitches and continue in colour B.

1

2

For example, if the pattern says 'using yarn A, 4 dc, using yarn B, 20 dc', this means that you need to work 1 double crochet into each of the 4 stitches using yarn A, then when you reach the last of the 4 stitches, use yarn B for the final yarn over, and continue to work double crochet in each of the next 20 stitches.

You should follow the same steps to change yarn when you reach the end of a ball. In this case the colour will stay the same.

In some patterns, the colours change quite often. I suggest three different methods for dealing with the yarns set aside while you are working in another colour.

- When alternating colours takes place close by (when 1 to 5 stitches separate the two colours, **1**): leave yarn A inside the piece while you crochet with yarn B. When you need to go back to yarn A, simply pick up the yarn to finish the last round in yarn B.

1

2

NOTE

Do not pull too hard on yarn A as you work: it should strand loosely across the back of the work so it does not pull it out of shape.

- When the colour changes are some distance apart (more than 5 stitches between the two colours, **2**): cut the yarn (leaving a tail of around 2cm/¾in) and knot the different colours together using a double knot.
- When you are crocheting stripes and the colours change on each round, do not cut the yarn: keep it inside the work until it is time to use it again.

When you are working in a spiral and need to change colour, it is normal that the colour change is slightly staggered between the rounds (see opposite). I do not try to make this staggered line invisible, but I position it on the back or side of the toy, or I sew the arms or legs on to it in order to make it less obvious.

JOINING TWO IDENTICAL PARTS

In the majority of my patterns, you will have to join two identical parts – for example, two legs. As you are working in spiral rounds, one round is always slightly staggered in comparison with the previous one. Work into the stitch that follows the last stitch in the previous round, in order to compensate (**1**). This will be the first stitch of the next round (**2**).

1

2

ATTACHING YARN TO THE FRONT LOOP

To make attractive borders for the clothes of soft toys, you can attach yarn to the front loop of the round earmarked for this purpose.

1 Insert the hook into the stitch (**1**).

2 Draw the new yarn you want to use through the stitch (**2**).

3 Continue working in accordance with the instructions in the pattern.

1

2

CUTTING THE YARN TO FASTEN OFF

When you finish a piece, you need to cut the yarn and add the finishing touches.

1 After you have crocheted the last stitch of the piece, cut the yarn (**1**).

2 Pass the end of the yarn through the loop on the hook and pull firmly (**2**).

1

2

> **NOTE**
>
> **If you are going to use the tail of yarn at a later stage to sew the parts together, make sure you leave enough (generally 15–20cm/6–8in).**

MAKING AN INVISIBLE JOIN

When you have cut the yarn and pulled it through the last stitch, you have a sort of chain stitch. For a neater finish, and a perfectly circular shape, you need this stitch to be incorporated in the edge of the piece. This is called an 'invisible join'.

1 Thread the end of the yarn into a needle. Miss a stitch and insert the needle under both loops of the next stitch (**1**).

2 Insert the needle into the back loop of the stitch where the tail starts (**2**).

3 Pull gently on the yarn so the join looks like a stitch and becomes the same size as the stitches around it (**3**).

1

2

3

WEAVING IN YARN ENDS

ON AN UNSTUFFED PIECE

1 Thread the end of the yarn into a needle, then weave it through several stitches on the wrong side of the work (**1**).

2 If any excess yarn remains cut it off flush against the back (**2**).

1

2

ON A STUFFED PIECE

1 Thread the end of the yarn into a needle, then insert it into the stuffed part, bringing it out and reinserting in different locations (**1 and 2**) until the tail is very short.

2 Cut off flush (**3**).

1

2

3

TYING OFF THE REMAINING STITCHES

When you are working the last round of a circular design there is often a small hole to fill.

1 Work the last stitch, cut the yarn and thread it onto a needle.

2 Insert the from outside to inside through the front loops of each stitch of the last round (**1**).

3 Pull gently on the yarn to draw the hole closed (**2**), then weave in or leave according to the instructions of the pattern.

1

2

SEWING THE PIECES TOGETHER

Once you have completed all the parts in the pattern, you then need to sew them together using a yarn needle. I use three types of stitches for making up: back stitch, mattress stitch and straight stitch.

- **Back stitch** for sewing pieces one on top of the other (such as a nose onto a head).

1 Position the pieces wrong side to right side. Insert the needle into the first stitch, passing it through both layers and reinsert the needle from back to front coming out in the next stitch (**1**).

2 Insert the needle into the previous stitch, passing it through both pieces (**2**).

3 Repeat stages 1 and 2 all the way round (**3**).

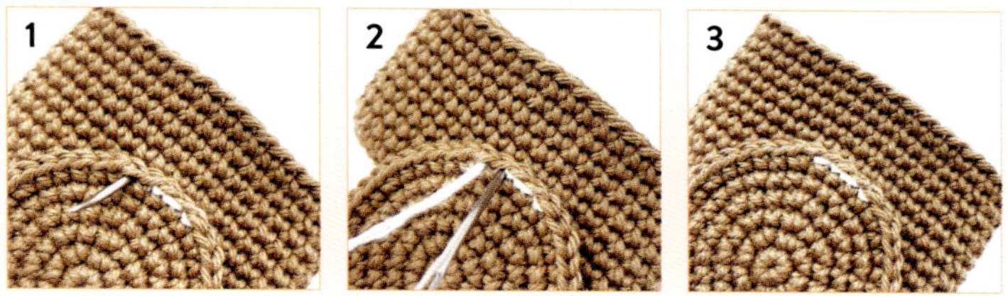

- **Mattress stitch** gives an almost invisible seam as long as you do not pull too hard on the yarn. I use it to sew together two open pieces, such as the head to the body.

1 Insert the needle into the relevant stitch, from front to back, where the yarn comes out and under the next stitch (**1**).

2 On the other piece, insert it from front to back, at the point where the yarn comes out and under the next stitch (**2**).

3 Repeat stages 1 and 2 as many times as necessary (**3**).

- **Straight stitch** for sewing a flat piece to a stuffed piece (such as an arm to a body) or for sewing an open piece to a stuffed piece (such as ears to a head, or a tail to a body).

1 Insert the needle into a stitch on the open piece, from the back of the work to the front (**1**).

2 Insert the needle into the corresponding stitch on the other piece, from right side to wrong, then bring it out in the next stitch (**2**).

3 Repeat stages 1 and 2 all round (**3**).

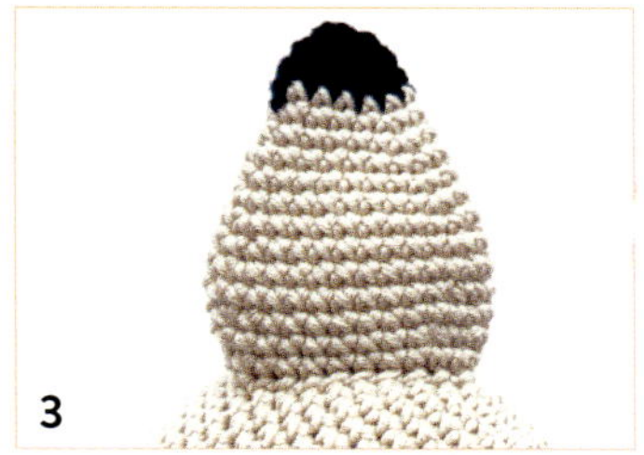

GENERAL POINTS ABOUT MAKING UP

- Make sure you keep a sufficiently long piece of yarn on at least one of the pieces to be made up, so you can work the entire seam between the two. If both pieces are open (such as the body and the head), I prefer to leave a length of yarn on each piece. Use the yarn from one of the pieces for making up; the other can be used to add a few additional stitches to reinforce the seams.
- First of all, pin all the pieces together (**1**). This allows you to check the positioning of symmetrical pieces (arms, legs, ears, etc.) in advance.
- When you sew the head to the body: start with the yarn in the middle of the neck so you can be sure that the head is sits straight (**2**).
- When the head and the body are different colours: sew the two loops of the head into the back loops of the body (or sew the two loops of body into the back loops of the head) to make a neat join (**3**).
- For a piece stuffed with wadding (batting), try to add a little more stuffing just before sewing it closed to ensure a nice shape.

EMBROIDERY STITCHES

STRAIGHT STITCH

I do most of my embroidery in straight stitch.

1 Insert the needle between the stitches, from the back to the front of the work, where you want the embroidery stitch to start, and pull through (**1**).

2 Reinsert the needle into the stitch, from the back to the front, bringing it out again where the next stitch will begin (**2**). The needle is once again on the right side of the work.

3 Repeat for each stitch (**3 and 4**).

FRENCH KNOT

French knots work very well on soft toys and add a little bit of texture.

1 Insert the needle from wrong side to right side, and pull through (**1**).

2 Wrap the yarn around the needle (**2**); the more turns you do, the bigger the knot will be.

3 Insert close to the place where you brought the needle out (**3**).

4 Pull gently on the yarn, letting the loops slide along it gently (**4**). Make sure you do not pull too hard, as the knot may come undone or be pulled through the stitches.

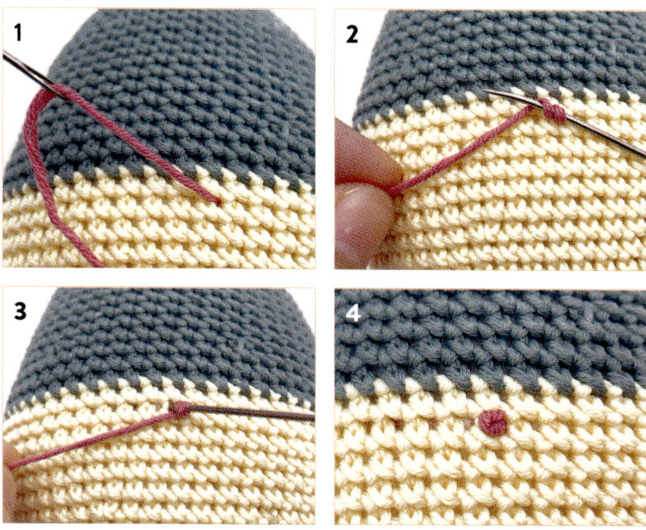

HOW TO READ MY PATTERNS

ABBREVIATIONS AND SYMBOLS

ABBREVIATIONS	
st(s)	stitch(es)
ch	chain
sl st	slip stitch
dc	double crochet (US single crochet)
htr	half-treble (US half-double)
tr	treble (US double)
dtr	double treble (US treble)
TBL	through back loop
TFL	through front loop
PC	popcorn stitch
sk	skip (US miss)

SYMBOLS	
( )	Number of stitches at the end of each round.
()	Instructions to repeat as many times as indicated.
( )	Series of actions to be performed into a single stitch.

DIFFICULTY LEVELS	
*	**Easy:** infrequent colour changes, simple shapes and detailing. Quick project.
**	**Intermediate:** more complex colour changes. More complicated shape. More details and pieces to sew. Longer project.
***	**Advanced:** multiple colour changes, unusual shapes and details. Numerous details. Long project.

INSTRUCTIONS

Here are a few examples to help you understand the instructions in this book.

EXAMPLE 1 (ANNA – BODY – PAGE 78)

Round 19: using yarn A, (5 dc, dc2tog) TBL three times (18 sts).
> To work round 19, only work into the back loops (see technique for working into back loops on page 16) and repeat three times: work one double crochet into each of the next five stitches, then work a decrease. At end of round 19, you will have 18 double crochet stitches.

EXAMPLE 2 (CHI THE KITTEN – HEAD AND BODY – PAGE 87)

Round 4: 2 dc, 2 dc into next st, (using yarn A, 2 dc, using yarn D, 2 dc into next st) three times, using yarn A, (2 dc, 2 dc into next st) three times (28 sts).
> Alternate mustard and yellow (see page 17 for how to change colour and what to do with the yarn that is set aside while you work the other colour). Make sure you work the correct number of stitches in each colour.

2 dc, 2 dc into next st
> Using the yarn from the previous round (yarn A), work a double crochet into each of the two next stitches, then work an increase.

(using yarn A, 2 dc, using yarn D, 2 dc into next st) three times
> Repeat the instructions in brackets three times: using yarn A, work a double crochet in each of the next 2 stitches, then when you reach the last of the 2 stitches, work the last yarn over using yarn D; work an increase into the next stitch, a double crochet in each of the next 3 stitches, then when you reach the last of the 3 stitches, work the last yarn over with yarn A.

using yarn A, (2 dc, 2 dc into next st) three times (28 sts).
> Using the yellow yarn, repeat the following three times: a double crochet into each of the next 2 stitches, then work an increase. At the end of the round, you will have 28 double crochet stitches.

EXAMPLE 3 (LEON THE BEAR – HAT – PAGE 33)

Round 3 (holes for ears): 2 ch, 18 tr, 8 ch, miss 8 sts (first hole for ear, 21), 12 tr, 8 ch, miss 8 sts (second hole for ear), 18 tr, join into top of first st (64 sts).
> The chain stitches at the start of each row do not count as 1 tr (see technique for working in joined rounds on page 15).

2 ch, 18 tr
> Round 3 allows you to create the openings so the bear's ears can poke out of the crocheted hat. Work 2 chain stitches, then the first treble into the same stitch as the chain stitches at the start of the row, then work a treble in each of the next 17 stitches.

8 ch, miss 8 sts (first hole for ear, 21).
> Work 8 chain stitches, miss the next 8 stitches, then work into the ninth stitch (from the last stitch worked). When you have done so, take a look at photo 21 to see if it looks right. You have formed the first hole in the hat.

12 tr
> Work a treble in each of the next 12 stitches.
8 ch, miss 8 sts (second ear hole), 18 tr, join with sl st

8 ch, miss 8 sts (second hole for ear), 18 tr, join into top of first st (64 sts).
> Work 8 chain stitches, miss the next 8 stitches, then work into the ninth stitch (from the last stitch worked). Then work a treble into each of the next 18 stitches. Join the round with a slip stitch into the first stitch of the round, this slip stitch does not count in the total stitch count for the round. At end of round 3, you will have 64 stitches.

the designs

LEON *the polar bear*

DIFFICULTY
***

Size: 24cm (9½in)

What you need

- Basic kit (see pages 8–9)
- 2.5mm (UK 12/13, US 1/2) crochet hook
- 2 safety eyes, 7mm (¼in)
- Paper (for the letters)
- Pompom maker, 3.5cm (1½in)
- Black embroidery thread

Yarns (see pages 6–7 for substitution information)

- DMC Happy Cotton
  - 1 ball each in red 789 (A) and black 775 (B)
  - 3 balls in cream 761 (C)
- DMC Woolly
  - 1 ball each in green 086 (D) and yellow 959 (E)
- DMC Woolly Chic
  - 1 ball each in white 01 (F) and blue 073 (G)
- DMC Lumina
  - small amount in L3821 (H)

Leon is a polar bear who lives at the North Pole. Every year, as Christmas approaches, he helps Santa Claus's elves to gather and sort out the children's letters to make sure not a single one is missed. A mug of hot chocolate helps him to keep warm on chilly days!

HEAD

Round 1: using yarn C, 8 dc into an adjustable ring (8 sts).
Round 2: 2 dc into each st around (16 sts).
Round 3: (1 dc, 2 dc in next st) eight times (24 sts).
Round 4: (2 dc, 2 dc in next st) eight times (32 sts).
Round 5: 1 dc, 2 dc in next st (3 dc, 2 dc in next st) seven times, 2 dc (40 sts).
Round 6: (4 dc, 2 dc in next st) eight times (48 sts).
Rounds 7–14 (8 rounds): 1 dc into each st around (48 sts).
Round 15: 23 dc, 2 dc in next st, 24 dc (49 sts).
Round 16: 16 dc, (2 dc in next st, 1 dc) twice, 3 dc, (2 dc in next st) twice, 4 dc, (2 dc in next st, 1 dc) twice, 16 dc (55 sts).
Round 17: 26 dc, 2 dc in next st, 28 dc (56 sts).
Rounds 18–20 (3 rounds): 1 dc into each st around (56 sts).
Round 21: 27 dc, dc2tog, 27 dc (55 sts).
Round 22: 1 dc into each st around (55 sts).
Round 23: 26 dc, dc2tog, 27 dc (54 sts).
Round 24: (7 dc, dc2tog) six times (48 sts).

Insert eyes between rounds 15 and 16. The first eye goes between sts 19 and 20, the second between sts 28 and 29 of the round.
Start stuffing the head, then continue stuffing as you go.
Round 25: 3 dc, dc2tog, (6 dc, 1 dc2tog) five times, 3 dc (42 sts).
Round 26: (5 dc, dc2tog) six times (36 sts).
Round 27: 2 dc, dc2tog, (4 dc, dc2tog) five times, 2 dc (30 sts).
Cut yarn, leaving a long enough tail for making up.
Using black embroidery thread, embroider a nose and mouth between the eyes, over rounds 17 and 20, then embroider eyebrows two rounds above each eye (**1**).

1

ARM (make 2)

Round 1: using yarn C, 7 dc into an adjustable ring (7 sts).
Round 2: (2 dc into next st) seven times (14 sts).
Rounds 3–6 (4 rounds): 1 dc into each st around (14 sts).
At end of round 6, switch to yarn G and cut yarn C. Start stuffing the arm, then continue stuffing as you go.
Round 7: using yarn G, 1 dc TBL of each st around (14 sts).
Rounds 8–11 (4 rounds): 1 dc into each st around (14 sts).
At end of round 11, switch to yarn D.
Rounds 12–14 (3 rounds): using yarn D, into each st around (14 sts).
At end of round 13, switch to yarn G and cut yarn D.
Rounds 15 and 16 (2 rounds): using yarn G, 1 dc into each st around (14 sts).
Fold the arm flat and line up the stitches on both sides of the opening (**2**). Work 1 dc in each pair of sts opposite each other along the top to close (7 sts).
Cut yarn, leaving a long enough tail for making up.

2

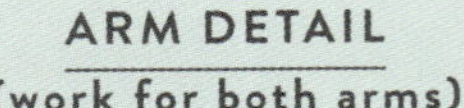

ARM DETAIL (work for both arms)

Turn the arm. Using yarn D and working TFL of round 6, insert hook into last st of round and draw through yarn D (3), 1 sl st into each st to end of round (14 sts). Cut yarn and weave in end (4).

3

4

LEG (make 2)

FIRST LEG

Using yarn B, 6 ch. The leg is worked in rounds around this foundation ch.
Round 1: starting in second ch from hook and working TFL, 2 dc into same st, 1 dc into each of next 3 sts, 4 dc into last st. Continue on other side: 1 dc into each of next 3 sts, 2 dc into next st (14 sts).
Round 2: 1 dc, 2 dc into next st, 3 dc, 2 dc into next st, 2 dc, 2 dc into next st, 3 dc, 2 dc into next st, 1 dc (18 sts).
Round 3: 1 dc, 2 dc into next st, 5 dc, 2 dc into next st, 2 dc, 2 dc into next st, 5 dc, 2 dc into next st, 1 dc (22 sts).
Round 4: (2 dc into next st, 1 sts) twice, 5 dc, (2 dc into next st, 1 sts) three times, 5 dc, 2 dc into next st, 1 dc (28 sts).
Round 5: 1 dc TBL of each st around (28 sts).
Round 6: 1 dc into each st around (28 sts).
Round 7: 12 dc, (dc2tog, 1 sts) three times, 7 dc (25 sts).
Round 8: 8 dc, (dc2tog, 1 sts) four times, 5 dc (21 sts).
Round 9: 7 dc, (dc2tog, 1 sts) three times, 5 dc (18 sts).
Round 10: (5 dc, 2 dc into next st) three times (21 sts).
Round 11: 1 dc into each st around (21 sts).
At end of round 11, switch to yarn C, leave yarn B on outside of leg to work boot detail (**5**) later.
Round 12: 1 dc TBL of each st around (21 sts).
Round 13: 16 dc (16 sts). Stop this round here, leaving 5 sts unworked. Cut yarn C, and stuff the leg.

SECOND LEG

Using yarn B, 6 ch.
Rounds 1–12 (12 rounds): as for rounds 1–12 of first leg.
Round 13: 1 dc into each st around (21 sts).
Round 14: 6 dc (6 sts). Stop this round here, leaving 15 sts unworked.

5

Do not cut yarn after last round; it will be used to crochet the legs together and make the body.

BODY

Continuing with yarn C and starting with the second leg (**9**), 1 ch and 1 dc to join it to the first leg (see page 18); this will be the first stitch of the body (**10**).

Continue forming the body from the two joined legs.

Round 1: 1 dc into each st of first leg, 1 dc into ch, 1 dc into each st of second leg, 1 dc TBL of ch (44 sts).

Round 2: (10 dc, 2 dc into next st) four times (48 sts).

Rounds 3–8 (**6 rounds**)**:** 1 dc into each st around (48 sts).

At end of round 8, work another 12 dc and move marker (if using) to last st worked (new end of round). Switch to yarn G (**11**) and cut yarn C.

Start stuffing the body, then continue stuffing as you go.

Round 9: 1 dc TBL of each st around (48 sts).

Rounds 10–13 (**4 rounds**)**:** 1 dc into each st around (48 sts).

Round 14: 1 dc, (using yarn D, 1 dc, using yarn G, 3 dc) eleven times, using yarn D, 1 dc, using yarn G, 2 dc (48 sts).

Round 15: (using yarn D, 3 dc, using yarn G, 1 dc) twelve times (48 sts).

Round 16: continuing with yarn G, 1 dc into each st around (48 sts).

Round 17: (5 dc, dc2tog) three times, 27 dc (45 sts).

At end of round 17, switch to yarn D.

Round 18: 1 dc into each st around (45 sts).

Round 19: 2 dc, (using yarn G, 1 dc, using yarn D, 4 dc) eight times, using yarn G, 1 dc, using yarn D, 2 dc (45 sts).

Round 20: 1 dc into each st around (45 sts).

At end of round 20, switch to yarn G.

Round 21: (4 dc, dc2tog) three times, 27 dc (42 sts).

Round 22: 1 dc into each st around (42 sts).

At end of round 22, switch to yarn D.

Round 23: (5 dc, dc2tog) six times (36 sts).

At end of round 23, switch to yarn G and cut yarn D.

Round 24: 1 dc into each st around (36 sts).

Round 25: (4 dc, dc2tog) six times (30 sts).

Cut yarn, leaving a long enough tail for making up.

See right for sweater detail.

9

10

11

BOOT DETAIL
(work for both legs)

1. Turn the leg. Using yarn B and working TFL of round 11, insert hook into last st of round and draw through yarn B (6), 1 sl st into each st to end of round (21 sts). Cut yarn and weave in end.

2. Working TFL of round 4, insert hook into last st of round and draw through yarn B (7), 1 sl st into each st to end of round (28 sl sts). Cut yarn and weave in end (8).

6

7

8

EAR (make 2)

Round 1: using yarn C, 6 dc into an adjustable ring (6 sts).
Round 2: (2 dc into next st) six times (12 sts).
Round 3: (1 dc, 2 dc into next st) six times (18 sts).
Rounds 4–6 (3 rounds): 1 dc into each st around (18 sts).
Cut yarn, leaving a long enough tail for making up (**14**).

TAIL

Round 1: using yarn C, 6 dc into an adjustable ring (6 sts).
Round 2: (2 dc into next st) six times (12 sts).
Round 3: (1 dc, 2 dc into next st) six times (18 sts).
Rounds 4–6 (3 rounds): 1 dc into each st around (18 sts).
Stuff the tail.
Round 7: (1 dc, dc2tog) six times (12 sts).
Round 8: (dc2tog, 1 dc) four times (8 sts).
Cut yarn, leaving a long enough tail for making up (**14**).

14

15

MAKING UP

Pin the ears between rounds 5 and 9 of the head (**15**), then sew on. Apply pink blusher to the cheeks and ears (**16**).
Sew on the arms 2 rounds below the last (top) round of the body (**17**).
Sew the tail to the middle of the back, 1 row below the sweater (**18**).
Attach the head, sewing into the back loops of the last round of the body, adding a little more stuffing just before closing up (**19**).

16

17

18

19

SWEATER DETAIL

1. Turn the body. Using yarn D and working TFL of round 8, insert hook into last st of round and draw through yarn D (**12**), 1 sl st into each st to end of round (48 sts). Cut yarn and weave in end.
2. Using yarn D, embroider little dots on round 12, using French knots (see page 23) (**13**).

12

13

ACCESSORIES

HAT

Using yarn A, 4 ch. The hat is worked in rows from this foundation ch.

Row 1: starting in second ch from hook, 3 dc (3 sts).

Row 2: 1 ch, turn, 3 dc (3 sts).

Row 3: 1 dc TBL of each st, 1 ch, turn, 3 dc (3 sts).

Rows 4–63 (**60 rows**): rep rows 2 and 3 thirty more times.

Row 64: 1 ch, turn, 3 dc (3 sts).

At end of row 64, join into top of first st to row 1 to complete brim of hat.

Continue working hat in joined rounds. 1-ch or 2-ch starting chs do not count as sts.

Round 1: 2 ch, 1 tr into each st, join into top of first st (64 sts).

Round 2: 1 ch, 1 dc into each st, join into top of first st (64 sts).

Round 3 (**holes for ears**): 2 ch, 18 tr, 8 ch, miss 8 sts (first hole for ear, **21**), 12 tr, 8 ch, miss 8 sts (second hole for ear), 18 tr, join into top of first st (64 sts).

21

20

Round 4: 1 ch, 1 dc into each st around, join into top of first st (64 sts).

Round 5: 2 ch, 1 tr into each st around, join into top of first st (64 tr).

Round 6: 1 ch, (6 dc, dc2tog) eight times, join into top of first st (56 sts).

Round 7: 2 ch, 1 tr into each st around, join into top of first st (56 tr).

Round 8: 1 ch, (5 dc, dc2tog) eight times, join into top of first st (48 sts).

Round 9: 2 ch, 1 tr into each st around, join into top of first st (48 tr).

Round 10: 1 ch, (4 dc, dc2tog) eight times, join into top of first st (40 sts).

22

23

24

25

Cut yarn, leaving a long enough tail for making up.

Sew rows 1 and 64 together to complete the brim of the hat (**22 and 23**).

Sew round 10 of the hat closed (**24 and 25**).

Using a pompom maker and yarn F, make a 3.5cm (1½in) pompom then sew on to the hat. Using yarn H, embroider little hearts on the hat (**26**).

SCARF

Using yarn A, 102 ch. Starting in third ch from hook, 1 htr TFL of each of the next 99 sts, 3 htr into last st. Continuing on other side, 1 htr into other loop of each of next 98 sts, 2 htr into last st, join into top of first st (202 sts).

Cut yarn and weave in end (**27**).

26

27

BAG

Using yarn E, 10 ch. The bag is worked in rounds around this foundation ch.
Round 1: starting in second ch from hook, 2 dc TFL of same st, 1 dc, 2 dc TFL of same st of next 7 sts, 4 dc into last st. Continue on other side side, working 1 dc into other loop of each of next 7 sts, 2 dc into next st (22 sts).
Round 2: 1 dc, 2 dc into next st, 7 dc, 2 dc into next st, 2 dc, 2 dc into next st, 7 dc, 2 dc into next st, 1 dc (26 sts).
Round 3: 1 sl st into each st around (26 sts).
Round 4: 1 dc TBL of each st around (26 sts).
Rounds 5–9 (5 rounds): 1 dc into each st around (26 sts).
Round 10: 13 dc, 51 ch (**28**) then, starting in second ch from hook, 1 sl st into each of next 50 sts (strap); continuing along top of bag (**29**), 13 dc.
Cut yarn, leaving a long enough tail for making up.
Sew the strap to the bag (**30**).
Cut the paper into the different letter shapes (**31**).

28

29

30

31

ALEX *the gingerbread man*

DIFFICULTY
*

Sizes: 9cm (3½in) for the gingerbread man and 11cm (4¼in) for the Christmas tree

What you need

- Basic kit (see pages 8–9)
- 2.5mm (UK 12/13, US 1/2) crochet hook
- Ribbon in colour of choice
- Black embroidery thread

Yarns (see pages 6 and 7 for substitution information)

- DMC Happy Cotton
  - 1 ball in beige 776 (A)
  - small amounts in pink 755 (B), dark red 791 (C) and red 789 (D)
- DMC Natura Just Cotton
  - small amounts in white N01 (E), green N14 (F) and blue N878 (G)
- DMC Woolly
  - 1 ball in green 082 (H)
  - small amount in yellow 091 (I)
- DMC Woolly Chic
  - small amounts in pink 045 (J) and blue 073 (K)
- DMC Knitty 4
  - small amount in brown 947 (L)
- DMC Lumina
  - small amount in L3821 (M)

Alex the gingerbread man, lives in a mysterious house where all the presents come from. He and the elves wrap thousands of presents each day. If there were a competition for wrapping presents, Alex would definitely be the world champion!

GINGERBREAD MAN

ARM (make 2)

Round 1: using yarn A, 8 dc into an adjustable ring (8 sts).
Round 2: (2 dc into next st, 3 dc) twice (10 sts).
Rounds 3–5 (3 rounds): 1 dc into each st around (10 sts).
Cut yarn, leaving a long enough tail for making up.
Stuff the arms.
Using yarn E, embroider the detail on round 3 (**1**).

1

LEG (make 2)

Round 1: using yarn A, 8 dc into an adjustable ring (8 sts).
Round 2: (2 dc into next st, 3 dc) twice (10 sts).
Rounds 3–6 (4 rounds): 1 dc into each st around (10 sts).
Cut yarn at end of first leg.
At end of second leg, do not cut yarn; you will use it to join the two legs and work the body (**2**).

HEAD AND BODY

The body is worked from the two joined legs.
Continuing with yarn A and starting with the second leg, 1 dc to join it to the first leg (see page 18); this will be the first stitch of the body (**3**).
Round 1: 1 dc into each st of first leg, 1 dc into each st of the leg (20 sts).
Start stuffing the legs and the body, then continue stuffing as you go.
Rounds 2–9 (8 rounds): 1 dc into each st around (20 sts).
Round 10: 5 dc, dc2tog, 8 dc, dc2tog, 3 dc (18 sts).
Round 11: (1 dc, dc2tog) six times (12 sts).
Round 12: 1 sl st into each st around (12 sl st).
Round 13: (1 dc, 2 dc into next st) six times (18 sts).
Round 14: 1 dc, 2 dc into next st, (2 dc, 2 dc into next st) five times, 1 dc (24 sts).
Rounds 15–22 (8 rounds): 1 dc each st around (24 sts).
Round 23: (2 dc, dc2tog) six times (18 sts).
Round 24: (dc2tog, 1 dc) six times (12 sts).
Round 25: dc2tog six times (6 dc)
Finish stuffing the head. Fasten off and tie off remaining sts.

2

3

4

5

Using black embroidery thread, work the eyes on round 18, 4 sts apart.
Using yarn D, embroider the mouth between two eyes on round 17.
Apply pink blusher to the cheeks.
Using yarn E, embroider the detail on round 3 of each leg and round 22 of the head. Embroider two small buttons on the body (**4**).
Sew the arms to the body (**5**).

CHRISTMAS TREE

Round 1: using yarn H, 4 dc into an adjustable ring (4 sts).
Round 2: (2 dc into next st, 1 sl st) TBL twice (6 sts).
Round 3: (1 dc, 2 dc into next st) three times (9 sts).
Round 4: 1 dc TBL of each st around (9 sts).
Round 5: (2 dc, 2 dc into next st) three times (12 sts).
Round 6: 1 dc TBL of each st around (12 sts).
Round 7: (3 dc, 2 dc into next st) three times (15 sts).
Round 8: 1 dc TBL of each st around (15 sts).
Round 9: (4 dc, 2 dc into next st) three times (18 sts).
Start stuffing the Christmas tree, then continue stuffing as you go.
Round 10: 1 dc TBL of each st around (18 sts).
Round 11: (5 dc, 2 dc into next st) three times (21 sts).
Round 12: 1 dc TBL of each st (21 sts).
Round 13: (6 dc, 2 dc into next st) three times (24 sts).
Round 14: 1 dc TBL of each st around (24 sts).
Round 15: (7 dc, 2 dc into each st around) three times (27 sts).
Round 16: 1 dc TBL of each st around (27 sts).
Round 17: (8 dc, 2 dc into next st) three times (30 sts).
Round 18: 1 dc TBL of each st around (30 sts).
Round 19: (14 dc, 2 dc into next st) twice (32 sts).
Round 20: (2 dc, dc2tog) TBL eight times (24 sts).
Round 21: (dc2tog, 1 dc) eight times (16 sts).
Round 22: dc2tog eight times (8 sts).
At end of round 22, switch to yarn L and cut yarn H.
Round 23: using yarn L, 1 sl st into each st around (8 sts).
Rounds 24–27 (4 rounds): 1 dc into each st around (8 dc)
Finish stuffing. Fasten off and tie off remaining sts TFL of round 27.

6

7

8

9

10

NEEDLES

Turn the tree. Using yarn H and working TFL of rounds 1–19, insert hook into last st of round 1 and draw through yarn H (**6**), (3 ch, 1 sl st into next st); rep to end of round 19.
Cut yarn and weave in end.
Using yarn M, embroider baubles using French knots (see page 23) (**7**).

STAR (make 2)

Make 2 stars and sew together (**8**).
Round 1: using yarn I, 10 dc into an adjustable ring, join into top of first st (10 sts).
Round 2: move to 3 ch, then starting in second ch from hook, 1 sl st, 1 dc, miss 1 st, 1 sl st) five times. Five points of star made.
Cut yarn, leaving a long enough tail for making up.
Sew the two stars together (**9**).
Sew the finished star to the top of the tree (**10**).

PLANT POT

Round 1: using yarn C, 8 dc into an adjustable ring (8 sts).
Round 2: (2 dc into next st) eight times (16 sts).
Round 3: (1 dc, 2 dc into next st) eight times (24 sts).
Round 4: 1 dc TBL of each st around (24 sts).
Rounds 5–8 (4 rounds): 1 dc into each st around (24 sts).
At end of round 8, switch to yarn M and cut yarn C.
Round 9: using yarn M, 1 sl st into each st around (24 sts).
Cut yarn, leaving a long enough tail for embroidery.
Using yarn M, embroider the details on round 7.

RIM

Turn the plant pot. Using yarn C and working TFL of round 3, insert hook into last st of round and draw through yarn C (**11**), 1 sl st into each st to end of round (24 sts).
Cut yarn and weave in ends (**12**).

12

PRESENTS

Each present is shaped differently. They do not require much yarn, so you can use up offcuts from other projects. Make several in different colours, using different hook sizes depending on which yarn you are using, so you end up with lots of different versions.

BOW

Using yarn M, make an adjustable ring.
(2 ch, 3 tr, 2 ch, 1 sl st into ring) twice.
Pull to close ring.
Cut yarn, wrap it round the centre of the bow and pull tight. Fasten off and cut, leaving a long enough tail for making up (**13**).
This bow can be used to decorate all the types of present.

PRESENT 1

BOX

Box is worked in joined rounds. Starting chs do not count as sts.
Round 1: using yarn G, 8 dc into an adjustable ring, join with sl st into top of first st (8 sts).
Round 2: 1 ch, (1 dc, 3 dc into next st) four times, join with sl st into top of first st (16 sts).
Round 3: 1 ch, 2 dc, 3 dc into next st, (3 dc, 3 dc into next st) three times, 1 dc, join with sl st into top of first st (24 sts).
Round 4: 1 ch, 3 dc, 3 dc into next st, (5 dc, 3 dc into next st) three times, 2 dc, join with sl st into top of first st (32 sts).
Round 5: 1 ch, 1 dc TBL of each st around, join with sl st into top of first st (32 sts).
Rounds 6 and 7 (2 rounds): 1 ch, 1 dc into each st around, join with sl st into top of first st (32 sts).
Cut yarn, leaving a long enough tail for making up.

LID

Using yarn G, make an adjustable ring.
Rounds 1–4 (4 rounds): rep rounds 1–4 of box.
Round 5: 1 sl st TBL of each st around (32 sts).

11

13

14

15

16

Round 6: 1 dc TBL of each st around (32 sts).
Cut yarn, work an invisible join (see page 19) and weave in the end.
Fold and shape the corners of the box and its lid (**14**).
Stuff the box, place the lid on top (**15**), then sew together. Use a ribbon or a length of yarn to tie a bow around the present (**16**).

PRESENT 2

BOX

Using yarn F, make an adjustable ring.
Round 1: 8 dc into adjustable ring, join with sl st into top of first st (8 sts).
Round 2: 1 ch (does not count as st here and throughout), (1 dc, 3 dc into next st) four times, join with sl st into top of first st (16 sts).
Round 3: 1 ch, 2 dc, 3 dc into next st, (3 dc, 3 dc into next st) three times, 1 dc, join with sl st into top of first st (24 sts).
Round 4: 1 ch, 1 dc TBL of each st around, join with sl st into top of first st (24 sts).
Rounds 5–9 (5 rounds): 1 ch, 1 dc into each st, join with sl st into each st around (24 sts).
Cut yarn, leaving a long enough tail for making up.

LID

Using yarn F, make an adjustable ring.
Rounds 1–3 (3 rounds): as rounds 1–3 of box.
Round 4: 1 sl st TBL of each st around (24 sts).
Round 5: 1 dc TBL of each st around (24 sts).
Round 6: 1 dc into each st around (24 sts).
Cut yarn, work an invisible join (see page 19) and weave in end. Fold and shape the corners of the box and its lid. Using yarn M, embroider little hearts on the box (**17**).

17

18

Stuff the box, place the lid on it, then sew together.
Sew the bow to the lid (**18**).

PRESENT 3

BOX

Using yarn B, make an adjustable ring.
Rounds 1–9: as rounds 1–9 of box for Present 2.
Rounds 10–12 (3 rounds): 1 ch, 1 dc into each st around, join with sl st into top of first st (24 sts).
Cut yarn, leaving a long enough tail for making up.

LID

Work lid as for Present 2. Fold and shape the corners of the box and the lid. Using yarn M, embroider little decorative marks on the box.
Stuff the box, place the lid on it, then sew together. Using a ribbon or a length of yarn, tie a bow around the present (**19**).

19

PRESENT 4

BOX

Present 4 is worked in joined rounds. Starting chs do not count as sts.

Round 1: using yarn D, 8 dc into an adjustable ring, join with sl st into top of first st (8 sts).

Round 2: 1 ch, (2 dc into next st) eight times, join with sl st into top of first st (16 sts).

Round 3: 1 ch, 1 dc TBL of each st around, join with sl st into top of first st (16 sts).

Rounds 4–9 (6 rounds): 1 ch, 1 dc into each st around, join with sl st into top of first st (16 sts).

Cut yarn, leaving a long enough tail for making up.

LID

Using yarn D, make an adjustable ring.

Rounds 1 and 2 (2 rounds): as rounds 1 and 2 of box (16 sts).

Round 3: 1 sl st TBL of each st around (16 sl sts).

Round 4: 1 dc TBL of each st around (16 sts).

Cut yarn and work an invisible join (see page 19) (**20**).

Stuff the box, place the lid on it, then sew them together. Using yarn M, embroider lines on the box. Sew a bow to the lid (**21**).

PRESENT 5

Round 1: using yarn I or yarn J, 6 dc into an adjustable ring (6 sts).

Round 2: (2 dc into next st) six times (12 sts).

Round 3: (1 dc, 2 dc into next st) six times (18 sts).

Round 4: (2 dc, 2 dc into next st) six times (24 sts).

Round 5: 1 dc into each st around (24 sts).

Stuff the present.

Round 6: dc2tog twelve times (12 sts).

Round 7: (1 dc, dc2tog) four times (8 sts).

Round 8: (1 dc, 2 dc into next st) four times (12 sts).

Round 9: (2 ch, 1 sl st into next st) twelve times (36 sts).

Cut yarn, leaving a long enough tail for making up.

Sew around round 8 to close up the bag (**22**).

Using an offcut of yarn in a different colour, tie a bow around it (**23**).

PRESENT 6

Using yarn K, 8 ch. Present 6 is worked in rows from this foundation ch. Starting chs do not count as sts.

Row 1: starting in second ch from hook, 7 dc (7 sts).

Rows 2–9 (8 rows): 1 ch, turn, 1 dc into each st across (7 sts).

Cut yarn, leaving a long enough tail for making up (**24**).

Roll up the rectangle made and work a few stitches to join in the middle. Use an offcut of yarn in a different colour to form a bow (**25**).

20

22

24

21

23

25

THE *Christmas* TRAIN

DIFFICULTY
**

Size: 30cm (12in)

What you need

- Basic kit (see pages 8–9)
- 2.75mm (UK 12, US 2) crochet hook

Yarns (see pages 6 and 7 for substitution information)

- DMC Happy Cotton
  - 2 balls in red 791 (A)
  - 1 ball each in black 775 (B) and brown 777 (C)
- DMC Knitty 4
  - small amount in yellow 766 (D)
  - 1 ball in green 839 (E)
  - small amount in dark brown 947 (F)
- DMC Lumina
  - 1 ball in L3821 (G)

Once he's wrapped all the presents, Alex the gingerbread man uses a specially designed train to deliver them to the house where Santa Claus lives. The elves are waiting there to get the sack ready. He has also remembered to bring the Christmas tree – he chose the most beautiful one in his forest.

WHEEL (make 32 sections)

Each wheel consists of two sections sewn together.
Using yarn B, 8 dc into an adjustable ring (8 sts).
Cut yarn, leaving a long enough tail for making up (**1**).
Put two pieces on top of each other and sew them together (**2**).
The wheel is complete (**3**).
These wheels will be used for all sections of the train.

1

2

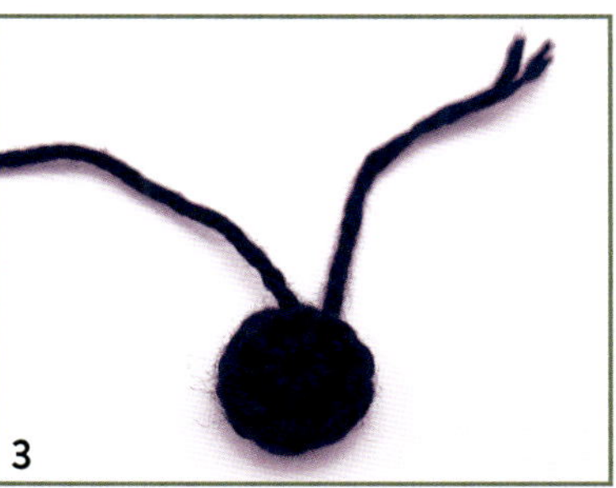

3

CENTRAL CARRIAGE
(make 2)

Each carriage is made up of two sections and four wheels.

UPPER SECTION

Using yarn A, 12 ch. The upper section is worked in rows from this foundation ch. Starting chs do not count as sts.

Row 1: starting in second ch from hook, 11 dc (11 sts).

Rows 2–9 (8 rows): 1 ch, turn, 1 dc into each st. Do not turn at end of row 9. (11 sts).

Row 10: continuing around main piece, work 2 htr into next st, 7 dc, 2 htr into next st, 9 dc, 2 htr into next st, 7 dc, 2 htr into next st, 9 dc, join with sl st into top of first st (40 sts) (**4, 5, 6, 7 and 8**).

This section is worked in joined rounds from this point on. Starting chs do not count as sts.

Rounds 11–14 (4 rounds): 1 ch, 1 dc into each st, join with sl st into top of first st (40 dc).

At end of round 14, switch to yarn G. Cut yarn A, leaving a long enough tail for making up.

Round 15: using yarn G, 1 sl st into each st around (40 sts).

Cut yarn, leaving a long enough tail for the embroidery.

Using yarn G, embroider the details on round 13 (**9**).

Fold and shape the corners of the carriage (**10 and 11**).

LOWER SECTION

Using yarn C, 12 ch.

Rows 1–9 (9 rows): as rows 1–9 of upper section. At end of row 9, do not turn (11 sts).

Row 10: continuing around main piece to first st of row 9, work 2 dc into next st, 7 dc, 2 dc into next st, 9 dc, 2 dc into next st, 7 dc, 2 dc into next st (31 sts).

Cut yarn, work an invisible join (see page 19) then weave in end (**12**).

Sew the two sections together (**13 and 14**).

Sew the four wheels under the lower section (**15**).

4

5

6

7

8

9

10

11

LAST CARRIAGE

The last carriage is made up of two sections and four wheels.

UPPER SECTION

Using yarn A, 18 ch. The upper section is worked in rows from this foundation ch. Starting chs do not count as sts.
Row 1: starting in second ch from hook, 17 dc (17 sts).
Rows 2–9 (8 rows): 1 ch, turn, 1 dc into each st. Do not turn at end of row 9 (17 sts).
Round 10: continuing around main piece, work 2 htr into next st, 7 dc, 2 htr into next st, 15 dc, 2 htr into next st, 7 dc, 2 htr into next st, 15 dc, join with sl st into top of first st (52 sts).
This section is worked in joined rounds from this point on. Starting chs do not count as sts.
Round 11: 1 ch, 1 dc into each st around, join with sl st into top of first st (52 sts).
At end of round 11, switch to yarn G.
Cut yarn A, leaving a long enough tail for making up.
Round 12: 1 dc into each st around (52 sts).
Cut yarn and weave in end.
Fold and shape the corners of the carriage.

LOWER SECTION

Using yarn C, 18 ch.
Rows 1–9 (9 rows): as rows 1–9 of upper section. At end of row 9, do not turn (17 sts).
Row 10: continuing around piece to first st of row 9, work 2 dc into next st, 7 dc, 2 dc into next st, 15 dc, 2 dc into next st, 7 dc, 2 dc into next st (37 sts).
Cut yarn, work an invisible join (see page 19) and weave in end (**16**).
Sew the two sections together, then sew the four wheels to the lower section (**17**).

12

13

14

15

16

LOCOMOTIVE

The locomotive comprises two upper sections, a lower section and four wheels.

UPPER SECTIONS

UPPER REAR SECTION

Using yarn A, 10 ch. The upper rear section is worked in rows from this foundation ch. Starting chs do not count as sts.

Row 1: starting in second ch from hook, 9 dc (9 sts).

Rows 2–9 (8 rows): 1 ch, turn, 1 dc into each st. Do not turn at end of row 9 (9 sts).

Round 10: continuing around piece, work (2 htr into the same st, 7 dc) four times, join with sl st into top of first st (36 sts).

This section is worked in joined rounds from this point on. Starting chs do not count as sts.

Rounds 11–20 (10 rounds): 1 ch, 1 dc into each st, join with sl st into top of first st (36 sts).

Cut yarn, leaving a long enough tail for making up.

Fold and shape the corners. Using yarn G, embroider the details (**18**).

UPPER FRONT SECTION

Round 1: using yarn A, 8 dc into an adjustable ring (8 sts).

Round 2: (2 dc into next st) eight times (16 sts).

Round 3: (1 dc, 2 dc into next st) eight times (24 sts).

Round 4: 1 dc TBL of each st around (24 sts).

Rounds 5–10 (6 rounds): 1 dc into each st around (24 sts).

Stuff this part.

Round 11: (1 dc, dc2tog) TBL eight times (16 sts).

Round 12: dc2tog eight times (8 sts).

Finish stuffing.

Cut yarn, leaving a long enough tail for making up and tie off remaining sts.

For detail for upper front section, see box above.

DETAIL

for upper front section

Using yarn G and working TFL of round 3, insert hook into last st of round and draw through yarn G (19), 1 sl st into each st to end of round (24 sts). Cut yarn, leaving a long enough tail for embroidery. Embroider lines (20).

19

20

17

18

CHIMNEY

Using yarn C, 10 ch and join with sl st, then 1 ch (**21**).

Rounds 1–3 (3 rounds): 1 dc into each st around (10 sts).

At end of round 3, switch to yarn G and cut yarn C, leaving a long enough tail for making up.

Round 4: (1 dc, 2 dc into next st) five times (15 sts).

Round 5: 1 dc into each st around (15 sts).

Cut yarn, work an invisible join (see page 19) then weave in end (**22**).

HEADLIGHT

Round 1: using yarn G, 8 dc into an adjustable ring (8 sts).

Rounds 2 and 3 (2 rounds): 1 dc into each st around (8 sts).

Cut yarn, leaving a long enough tail for making up (**22**).

Sew on headlight over round 1 and chimney over rounds 4–7 of upper front section (**23**).

Sew both upper sections together (**24**).

LOWER SECTION

Using yarn C, work two pieces as for the lower section of last carriage.

Sew all four wheels to one of the pieces (**25**), then sew the second piece to the first (**26**).

Sew the lower and upper sections together (**27**).

21

22

23

24

25

26

27

COUPLING (make 3)

Using yarn C, 10 ch.
Row 1: starting in second ch from hook, 9 sl st (9 sts).
Cut yarn, leaving a long enough tail for making up (**28**).
Sew each coupling between two carriages (**29 and 30**).
The Christmas tree is identical to the one on page 39, using yarn E and yarn F. The presents are identical to those on pages 40 to 42.
Cut a length of yarn D to tie the tree to the last carriage (**31 and 32**).

28

29

30

31

32

BOY ELVES

Difficulty *

Size: 14cm (5½in)

What you need

- Basic kit (see pages 8–9)
- 2.25mm (UK 13, US 1) crochet hook
- 2 safety eyes, 5mm (¼in)
- Black embroidery thread
- Brown embroidery thread

Yarns (see pages 6 and 7 for substitution information)

- DMC Natura Just Cotton
  - 1 ball each in beige N81 (A), red N555 (B) and green N14 (C)
  - small amount in brown N22 (D)
- DMC Lumina
  - small amount in L3821 (E)

The list given here is for the dark green shirt; to make the blue and light blue versions, see the alternative yarn and materials specifications on page 56.

Elves are Santa Claus's best partners. They might be small, but they are very strong, and have no problem carrying the presents about.

HEAD

Round 1: using yarn A, 7 dc into an adjustable ring (7 sts).
Round 2: (2 dc into next st) seven times (14 sts).
Round 3: (1 dc, 2 dc into next st) seven times (21 sts).
Round 4: (2 dc, 2 dc into next st) seven times (28 sts).
Round 5: 1 dc, 2 dc into next st, (3 dc, 2 dc into next st) six times, 2 dc (35 sts).
Round 6: (4 dc, 2 dc into next st) seven times (42 sts).
Rounds 7–15 (9 rounds): 1 dc into each st around (42 sts).
If using safety eyes, position them between rounds 10 and 11, 5 sts apart.
Start stuffing the head, then continue stuffing as you go.
Round 16: (4 dc, dc2tog) seven times (35 sts).
Round 17: 1 dc, dc2tog, (3 dc, dc2tog) six times, 2 dc (28 sts).
Round 18: (1 dc, dc2tog, 2 dc, dc2tog) four times (20 sts).
Cut yarn, leaving a long enough tail for making up.
Using brown embroidery thread, embroider eyebrows one round above each eye.
Using yarn A, embroider a nose between the eyes on round 11 (**1**).
Using yarn D, embroider hair between rounds 2 and 7 of the head (**2 and 3**).
To give a smiley expression, using black embroidery thread, embroider eyes over round 10, 3 sts wide and 4 sts apart (**4**).

1

2

3

4

5

6

7

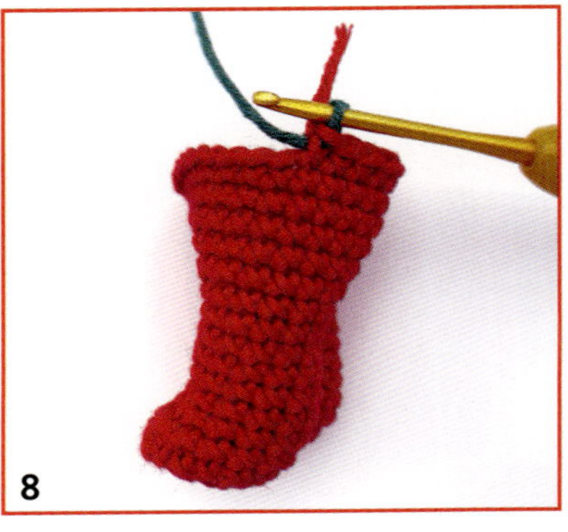
8

LEG (make 2)

FIRST LEG

Round 1: using yarn B, 8 dc into an adjustable ring (8 sts).
Round 2: (2 dc into next st) eight times (16 sts).
Round 3: 6 dc, 4 htr, 6 dc (16 sts).
Round 4: 6 dc, dc2tog twice, 6 dc (14 sts).
Round 5: 5 dc, dc2tog twice, 5 dc (12 sts).
Start stuffing the leg, then continue stuffing as you go.
Rounds 6 and 7 (2 rounds): 1 dc into each st around (12 sts).
Round 8: 10 dc (10 sts). Stop this round here, leaving 2 sts unworked.
Cut yarn.

SECOND LEG

Rounds 1–7 (7 rounds): as first leg.
Round 8: 1 dc into each st around (12 sts).
Round 9: 3 dc (3 sts). Stop this round here, leaving 9 sts unworked.
Do not cut yarn after last round; it will be used to crochet the legs together and make the body (**5**).

BODY

Continuing with yarn B and starting with the second leg, 1 ch (**6**) and 1 dc to join to the first leg (see page 18); this will be the first stitch of the body (**7**).
Round 1: 1 dc into each st of first leg, 1 dc TFL of ch, 1 dc into each st of second leg, 1 dc TBL of ch (26 sts).
Round 2: 24 dc, 2 dc into next st, 1 dc (27 sts).
Round 3: 2 dc into next st, 10 dc, 2 dc into next st, 1 dc, 2 dc into next st, 13 dc (30 sts).
Rounds 4–8 (5 rounds): 1 dc into each st around (30 sts).
At end of round 8, work 7 dc and move marker (if using) to last st worked (new end of round).
Switch to yarn C and cut yarn B (**8**).
Start stuffing the body, then continue stuffing as you go.
Round 9: 1 dc TBL of each st around (30 sts).

Rounds 10–13 (4 rounds): 1 dc into each st around (30 sts).
Round 14: (3 dc, dc2tog) six times (24 sts).
Round 15: 1 dc into each st around (24 sts).
Round 16: (4 dc, dc2tog) four times (20 sts).
Round 17 (neck): working TFL of round 16 and turning as you go (**9**), *miss 1 st, (1 htr, 1 tr, 2 ch, 1 sl st into first of 2 ch, 1 htr) into same st, miss 1 st, 1 sl st (**10**)*; rep from * to * five times.
Five 'petals' made.
Cut yarn and weave in end (**11**).

BOTTOM OF SHIRT

Turn body.
Round 1: using yarn C and working TFL of round 8, insert hook into last st of round (**12**), 1 ch, 1 dc into each st around (30 sts).
Round 2: 1 dc into each st around (30 sts).
Round 3: (2 dc into next st, 14 dc) twice (32 sts).
Round 4: *miss 1 st, (1 htr, 1 tr, 2 ch, 1 sl st into first ch, 1 htr) into same st, miss 1 st, 1 sl st*; rep from * to * eight times.
Eight 'petals' made.
Cut yarn and weave in end.
Using yarn E, embroider two little lines on the body for buttons (**13**).

10

11

12

9

13

ARM (make 2)

Round 1: using yarn A, 8 dc into an adjustable ring (8 sts).
Round 2: (2 dc into next st, 3 dc) twice (10 sts).
Rounds 3 and 4 (2 rounds): 1 dc into each st around (10 sts).
At end of round 4, switch to yarn C and cut yarn A.
Rounds 5–9 (5 rounds): using yarn C, 1 dc into each st around (10 sts).
Fold the arm flat and line up the stitches on both sides of the opening (**14**). Work 1 dc in each pair of sts opposite each other along the top to close (5 sts).
Cut yarn, leaving a long enough tail for making up (**15**).

14

15

EAR (make 2)

Round 1: using yarn A, 5 dc into an adjustable ring (5 sts).
Round 2: 2 dc into next st, 4 dc (6 sts).
Round 3: (2 dc, 2 dc into next st) twice (8 sts).
Round 4: (1 dc, 2 dc into next st) four times (12 sts).
Rounds 5–7 (3 rounds): 1 dc into each st around (12 sts).
Round 8: dc2tog six times (6 sts).
Cut yarn, leaving a long enough tail for making up (**16**).

16

HAT

Round 1: using yarn B, 6 dc into an adjustable ring (6 sts).
Round 2: 2 dc into next st, 5 dc (7 sts).
Round 3: 2 dc into next st, 6 dc (8 sts).
Round 4: (2 dc into next st, 3 dc) twice (10 sts).
Round 5: 1 dc into each st around (10 sts).
Round 6: (4 dc, 2 dc into next st) twice (12 sts).
Round 7: 1 dc into each st around (12 sts).
Round 8: (3 dc, 2 dc into next st) three times (15 sts).
Rounds 9 and 10 (2 rounds): 1 dc into each st around (15 sts).
Round 11: (4 dc, 2 dc into next st) three times (18 sts).
Round 12: 1 dc into each st around (18 sts).
Round 13: (5 dc, 2 dc into next st) three times (21 sts).
Round 14: (6 dc, 2 dc into next st) three times (24 sts).
Round 15: 1 dc into each st around (24 sts).
Round 16: (3 dc, 2 dc into next st) six times (30 sts).
Round 17: 1 dc into st around (30 sts).
Round 18: (4 dc, 2 dc into next st) six times (36 sts).
Rounds 19–24 (6 rounds): 1 dc into each st around (36 sts).
Cut yarn, leaving a long enough tail for making up (**17**).

17

MAKING UP

Pin the ears in place on either side of the head over rounds 10 and 11, approximately 5 sts from the eyes, then sew in place (**18**).
Sew the hat onto the head.
Sew on the arms 1 round below the neck.
Attach the head, sewing into the back loops of round 16 of the body, adding a little more stuffing just before closing up (**19**).
Apply pink blusher to the cheeks and inside the ears.

18

19

MAKING THE OTHER BOY ELVES

Here are the alternative colours for making the other boy elves — but there's nothing to stop you letting your imagination run wild!

	BLUE VERSION	LIGHT BLUE VERSION
Shirt	DMC Natura Just Cotton blue N878	DMC Natura Just Cotton teal N20
Hat and boots	DMC Natura Just Cotton red N555	DMC Natura Just Cotton red N23
Hair	DMC Natura Just Cotton brown N41	DMC Natura Just Cotton brown N41

GIRL ELVES

Size: 14cm (5½in)

What you need

- Basic kit (see pages 8–9)
- 2.25mm (UK 13, US 1) crochet hook
- Black embroidery thread
- Brown embroidery thread

Yarns (see pages 6 and 7 for substitution information)

- DMC Natura Just Cotton
  – 1 ball each in beige N81 (A), red N555 (B) and green N989 (C)
- DMC Knitty 4
  – small amount in brown 947 (D)
- DMC Lumina
  – small amount in L3821 (E)

The list given here is for the light green dress; to make the blue and dark green versions, see the alternative yarn and materials specifications on page 64.

Just like the boy elves, the girl elves are full of energy and raring to go. Each of them has a specific role and they work as a team very efficiently. Everything will be ready on time!

LEG (make 2)

FIRST LEG

Round 1: using yarn B, 8 dc into an adjustable ring (8 sts).
Round 2: (2 dc into next st) eight times (16 sts).
Round 3: 6 dc, 4 htr, 6 dc (16 sts).
Round 4: 6 dc, dc2tog twice, 6 dc (14 sts).
Round 5: 5 dc, dc2tog twice, 5 dc (12 sts).
Start stuffing the leg, then continue stuffing as you go.
Rounds 6 and 7 (2 rounds): 1 dc into st around (12 sts).
Round 8: 10 dc (10 sts). Stop this round here, leaving 2 sts unworked. Cut yarn.

SECOND LEG

Rounds 1–7 (7 rounds): as first leg.
Round 8: 1 dc into each st around (12 sts).
Round 9: 3 dc (3 sts). Stop this round here, leaving 9 sts unworked.
Do not cut yarn after last round; it will be used to crochet the legs together and make the body (**1**).

1

BODY

Continuing with yarn B and starting with the second leg, 1 ch (**2**) and 1 dc to join it to first leg (see page 18); this will be the first stitch of the body (**3**).
Round 1: 1 dc into each st of first leg, 1 dc TFL of ch, 1 dc into each st of second leg, 1 dc TBL of ch (26 sts).
Rounds 2–10 (9 rounds): 1 dc into each st around (26 sts).
Start stuffing the body, then continue stuffing as you go.
Round 11: 5 dc, dc2tog, 11 dc, dc2tog, 6 dc (24 sts).
Rounds 12–14 (3 rounds): 1 dc into each st around (24 sts).
At end of round 14, switch to yarn C and cut yarn B.
Round 15: using yarn C, 1 dc into each st around (24 sts).
Round 16: (4 dc, dc2tog) TBL four times (20 sts).
Do not cut yarn; you will use it to work the neck.

2

3

COLLAR

Round 1: continuing with yarn C and working TFL of round 16 (**4 and 5**), turn, 2 ch, (4 htr, 2 htr into next st) four times, join with 1 sl st into top of first st (24 sts).
Round 2: *miss 1 st, (1 htr, 1 tr, 2 ch, 1 sl st into first of 2 ch, 1 htr) into same st, miss 1 st, 1 sl st*, rep from * to * six times.
Six 'petals' made.
Cut yarn and weave in end (**6**).

DRESS

Round 1: using yarn C and working TFL of round 15, turn body, insert hook into last st of round and draw through yarn C (**7**), 2 ch, 1 htr into each st around (24 sts).
Round 2: 1 htr into each st around (24 sts).
Round 3: (3 htr, 2 htr into next st) six times (30 sts).
Round 4: 1 htr into each st around (30 sts).
Round 5: (4 htr, 2 htr into next st) six times (36 sts).
Rounds 6 and 7 (2 rounds): 1 htr into each each st around (36 sts).
Round 8: *miss 1 st, (1 htr, 1 tr, 2 ch, 1 sl st into first of 2 ch, 1 htr) into same st, miss 1 st, 1 sl st*, rep from * to * nine times.
Nine 'petals' made.
Cut yarn and weave in end.
Using yarn E, embroider dots on the dress using French knots (see page 23) (**8**).

4

6

5

7

8

ARM (make 2)

Round 1: using yarn A, 8 dc into an adjustable ring (8 sts).
Round 2: (2 dc into next st, 3 dc) twice (10 sts).
Rounds 3 and 4 (2 rounds): 1 dc into each st around (10 dc)
At end of round 4, switch to yarn B and cut yarn A.
Rounds 5–9 (5 rounds): 1 dc into each st around (10 sts).
Fold the arm flat and line up the stitches on both sides of the opening (**9**). Work 1 dc in each pair of sts opposite each other along the top to close (5 sts).
Cut yarn, leaving a long enough tail for making up (**10**).

EAR (make 2)

Round 1: using yarn A, 5 dc into an adjustable ring (5 sts).
Round 2: 2 dc into next st, 4 dc (6 sts).
Round 3: (2 dc, 2 dc into next st) twice (8 sts).
Round 4: (1 dc, 2 dc into next st) four times (12 sts).
Rounds 5–7 (3 rounds): 1 dc into each st around (12 sts).
Round 8: dc2tog six times (6 sts).
Cut yarn, leaving a long enough tail for making up (**11**).

HAT

Round 1: using yarn B, 6 dc into an adjustable ring (6 sts).
Round 2: 2 dc into next st, 5 dc (7 sts).
Round 3: 2 dc into next st, 6 dc (8 sts).
Round 4: (2 dc into next st, 3 dc) twice (10 sts).
Round 5: 1 dc into each st around (10 sts).
Round 6: (4 dc, 2 dc into next st) twice (12 sts).
Round 7: 1 dc into each st around (12 sts).
Round 8: (3 dc, 2 dc into next st) three times (15 sts).
Rounds 9 and 10 (2 rounds): 1 dc into each st around (15 sts).
Round 11: (4 dc, 2 dc into next st) three times (18 sts).
Round 12: 1 dc into each st around (18 sts).
Round 13: (5 dc, 2 dc into next st) three times (21 sts).
Round 14: (6 dc, 2 dc into next st) three times (24 sts).
Round 15: 1 dc into each st around (24 sts).
Round 16: (3 dc, 2 dc into next st) six times (30 sts).
Round 17: 1 dc into each st around (30 sts).
Round 18: (4 dc, 2 dc into next st) six times (36 sts).
Rounds 19–24 (6 rounds): 1 dc into each st around (36 sts).
Cut yarn, leaving a long enough tail for making up (**12**).

HEAD

Round 1: using yarn A, 7 dc into an adjustable ring (7 sts).
Round 2: (2 dc into next st) seven times (14 sts).
Round 3: (1 dc, 2 dc into next st) seven times (21 sts).
Round 4: (2 dc, 2 dc into next st) seven times (28 sts).
Round 5: 1 dc, 2 dc into next st, (3 dc, 2 dc into next st) six times, 2 dc (35 sts).
Round 6: (4 dc, 2 dc into next st) seven times (42 sts).
Rounds 7–15 (9 rounds): 1 dc into each st (42 sts).
Start stuffing the head, then continue stuffing as you go.
Round 16: (4 dc, dc2tog) seven times (35 sts).
Round 17: 1 dc, dc2tog, (3 dc, dc2tog) six times, 2 dc (28 sts).
Round 18: (1 dc, dc2tog, 2 dc, dc2tog) four times (20 sts).
Cut yarn, leaving a long enough tail for making up.

9

10

11

12

HAIR

Round 1: using yarn D, 7 dc into an adjustable ring (7 sts).
Round 2: (2 dc into next st) TFL seven times (14 sts).
Cut yarn, leaving a long enough tail for making up.
Cut 35 lengths of yarn D, approximately 10cm (4in) each (**13**). Attach each length of yarn TFL and TBL of each st of round 2 and TBL of each st of round 1 (**14, 15, 16, 17 and 18**).
Style hair with a comb (**19 and 20**).

13

14

15

16

17

18

19

20

MAKING UP

Sew on the arms 1 round below the neck.
Using black embroidery thread, embroider eyes over round 10, 4 sts apart. You can make the elves look playful (**21**) or happy (**22**).
Using brown embroidery thread, embroider eyebrows 2 rounds above each eye and a mouth between the eyes over round 12.
Pin the ears in place on either side of the head over rounds 10 and 11, approximately 5 sts from the eyes, then sew in place (**18**).

Apply pink blusher to the cheeks, and inside the ears (**21 and 22**).
Place the hair on the head, distributing it nicely across the rounds, with more at the back, then sew into place (**23, 24 and 25**).
Sew the hat to the head (**26**).
Use scissors to trim the hair to the desired length (**27**).

21

22

23

24

25

26

27

28

29

Attach the head, sewing into the back loops of round 16 of the body, adding a little more stuffing just before closing up.
You can also make bunches (**28**) or plaits (**29**).

MAKING THE OTHER GIRL ELVES

Here are the alternative colours for making the other girl elves – but there's nothing to stop you letting your imagination run wild!

	BLUE VERSION	DARK GREEN VERSION
Dress	DMC Natura Just Cotton blue N878	DMC Woolly green 082
Arms, hat and boots	DMC Natura Just Cotton red N23	DMC Natura Just Cotton red N555
Hair	DMC Natura Just Cotton brown N41	DMC Knitty 4 mustard 766

SANTA CLAUS *and his sack*

You have already heard so many magical stories about Santa Claus and some of you might even have seen him (I really hope to do so myself one day!). But did you know about his magic sack? It might look like a normal sack, but he can put as many presents in it as he likes. I bet it would be impossible to count them all.

DIFFICULTY
***

Size: 24cm (9½in)

What you need

- Basic kit (see pages 8–9)
- 2.5mm (UK 12/13, US 1/2) crochet hook (main hook – use this hook unless stated otherwise)
- 4mm (UK 8, US 6) crochet hook (for the moustache and beard)
- 2 safety eyes, 8mm (¼in)
- 2 safety eyes (or little buttons), 5mm (¼in)

Yarns (see pages 6 and 7 for substitution information)

- DMC Happy Cotton
  - 3 balls in red 789 (A)
  - 1 ball each in black 775 (B) and cream 761 (C)
  - small amount in brown 777 (D)
- DMC Woolly
  - 1 ball each in beige 044 (E) and yellow 959 (F)
- DMC Velvet
  - 1 ball in cream 004 (G)
- DMC Teddy
  - 1 ball in white 310 (H)
- DMC Lumina
  - small amount in L3821 (I)

HEAD

Round 1: using yarn E, 8 dc into an adjustable ring (8 sts).
Round 2: (2 dc into next st) eight times (16 sts).
Round 3: (1 dc, 2 dc into next st) eight times (24 sts).
Round 4: (2 dc, 2 dc into next st) eight times (32 sts).
Round 5: 1 dc, 2 dc into next st, (3 dc, 2 dc into next st) seven times, 2 dc (40 sts).
Round 6: (4 dc, 2 dc into next st) eight times (48 sts).
Rounds 7 and 8 (2 rounds): 1 dc into each st around (48 sts).
Round 9: (7 dc, 2 dc into next st) six times (54 sts).
Rounds 10–14 (5 rounds): 1 dc into each st around (54 sts).
Round 15: (8 dc, 2 dc into next st) six times (60 sts).
Rounds 16–19 (4 rounds): 1 dc into each st around (60 sts).
Round 20: (8 dc, dc2tog) six times (54 sts).
Round 21: 3 dc, dc2tog, (7 dc, dc2tog) five times, 4 dc (48 sts).
Round 22: (6 dc, dc2tog) six times (42 sts).
Insert 8mm (¼in) eyes between rounds 12 and 13, 8 sts apart.
Start stuffing the head, then continue stuffing as you go.
Round 23: 2 dc, dc2tog, (5 dc, dc2tog) five times, 3 dc (36 sts).
Round 24: (4 dc, dc2tog) six times (30 sts).
Cut yarn, leaving a long enough tail for making up.
Using yarn E, embroider eyelids above each eye (**1**).

EAR (make 2)

Using yarn E, work 2 ch, 5 tr, 2 ch, 1 sl st into an adjustable ring. Pull to close ring.
Cut yarn, leaving a long enough tail for making up (**2**).

NOSE

Round 1: using yarn E, 6 dc into an adjustable ring (6 sts).
Round 2: (2 dc into next st, 1 dc) three times (9 sts).
Round 3: 1 dc into each st around (9 sts).
Cut yarn, leaving a long enough tail for making up (**2**).

MOUSTACHE AND BEARD

MOUSTACHE

Using yarn G and 4mm (UK 8, US 6) crochet hook, 4 ch. Starting in second ch from hook, 1 sl st, 1 dc, 1 sl st, 4 ch, starting in second ch from hook, 1 sl st, 2 dc, 1 sl st, 1 sl st into first st of initial 4 ch. This sl st closes up the end completely to form the moustache.
Cut yarn, leaving a long enough tail for making up.

BEARD

Using yarn G and 4mm (UK 8, US 6) crochet hook, 16 ch. The beard is worked in rows from this foundation ch. Starting chs do not count as sts.
Row 1: starting in second ch from hook, 15 dc (15 sts).
Row 2: 1 ch, turn, miss first st, 14 dc (14 sts).
Row 3: 1 ch, turn, miss first st, 13 dc (13 sts).
Row 4: 1 ch, turn, miss first st, 12 dc (12 sts).
Cut yarn, leaving a long enough tail for making up (**3**).

1

2

3

HAT

Round 1: using yarn A, 6 dc into an adjustable ring (6 sts).
Round 2: (2 dc into next st, 1 sts) three times (9 sts).
Round 3: 1 dc into each st around (9 sts).
Round 4: (2 dc, 2 dc into next st) three times (12 sts).
Rounds 5 and 6 (2 rounds): 1 dc into each st around (12 sts).
Round 7: (3 dc, 2 dc into next st) three times (15 sts).
Rounds 8 and 9 (2 rounds): 1 dc into each st around (15 sts).
Round 10: (4 dc, 2 dc into next st) three times (18 sts).
Round 11: 1 dc into each st around (18 sts).
Round 12: (5 dc, 2 dc into next st) three times (21 sts).
Round 13: 1 dc into each st around (21 sts).
Round 14: (6 dc, 2 dc into next st) three times (24 sts).
Round 15: 1 dc into each st around (24 sts).
Round 16: (7 dc, 2 dc into next st) three times (27 sts).
Round 17: 1 dc into each st around (27 sts).
Round 18: (8 dc, 2 dc into next st) three times (30 sts).
Round 19: 1 dc into each st around (30 sts).
Round 20: (9 dc, 2 dc into next st) three times (33 sts).
Round 21: 1 dc into each st around (33 sts).
Round 22: (10 dc, 2 dc into next st) three times (36 dc).
Round 23: 1 dc into each st around (36 dc).
Round 24: (5 dc, 2 dc into next st) six times (42 dc).
Rounds 25–34 (10 rounds): 1 dc into each st around (42 sts).
At end of round 34, switch to yarn H and cut yarn A, leaving a long enough tail for making up.
Rounds 35–38 (4 rounds): using yarn H, 1 htr into each st around (42 sts).
Cut yarn H, leaving a long enough tail for making up.

POMPOM

Round 1: using yarn H, 6 dc into an adjustable ring (6 sts).
Round 2: (2 dc into next st) six times (12 sts).
Round 3: (2 dc into next st, 1 sts) six times (18 sts).
Round 4: 1 dc into each st around (18 sts).
Stuff the pompom.
Round 5: (1 dc, dc2tog) six times (12 sts).
Round 6: dc2tog six times (6 sts).
Cut yarn, leaving a long enough tail for making up and tie off remaining sts.
Sew pompom to top of hat (**4**).

4

5

6

7

MAKING UP THE HEAD

Pin the nose in place between the eyes and between rounds 13 and 15, and the ears on either side of the head between rounds 11 and 14, approximately 6 sts from the eyes (**5**); then sew on.
Pin the beard in place on the head (**6 and 7**), then sew on.
Sew on the moustache just below the nose. Using yarn G, embroider eyebrows two rounds above each eye.
Apply pink blusher to the cheeks, nose and ears (**8**).
Place the hat on Santa's head, pin in place, then fold it into shape and sew on (**9**).

ARM (make 2)

Round 1: using yarn C, 7 dc into an adjustable ring (7 sts).
Round 2: (2 dc into next st) seven times (14 sts).
Rounds 3 and 4 (2 rounds): 1 dc into each st around (14 sts).
Round 5: 5 dc, 1 PC, 8 dc (14 sts).
Round 6: 1 dc into each st around (14 sts).
At end of round 6, switch to yarn A, leaving yarn C on the outside of the arm to work the glove detail later (**10**).
Start stuffing the arm, then continue stuffing as you go.
Round 7: 1 dc TBL of each st around (14 sts).
Rounds 8–16 (9 rounds): 1 dc into each st around (14 dc).
Fold the arm flat and line up the stitches on both sides of the opening (**11**). Work 1 dc in each pair of sts opposite each other along the top to close (7 sts).
Cut yarn, leaving a long enough tail for making up.

GLOVE DETAIL
(work for both arms)

Using yarn C and working TFL of round 6, insert hook into first st of round and draw through yarn C (12), then 1 ch, 14 dc. Cut yarn, work an invisible join (see page 19) and weave in end (13).

12

13

8

9

10

11

LEG (make 2)

FIRST LEG

Using yarn B, 6 ch. The leg is worked in rounds around this foundation ch.
Round 1: starting in second ch from hook and working TFL, 2 dc into next st, 1 dc into each of next 3 sts, 4 dc into last st. Continuing in other loops of ch, 1 dc into each of next 3 sts, 2 dc into next st (14 sts).
Round 2: 1 dc, 2 dc into next st, 3 dc, 2 dc into next st, 2 dc, 2 dc into next st, 3 dc, 2 dc into next st, 1 dc (18 sts).
Round 3: 1 dc, 2 dc into next st, 5 dc, 2 dc into next st, 2 dc, 2 dc into next st, 5 dc, 2 dc into next st, 1 dc (22 sts).
Round 4: (2 dc into next st, 1 dc) twice, 5 dc, (2 dc into next st, 1 dc) three times, 5 dc, 2 dc into next st, 1 dc (28 sts).
Round 5: 1 dc TBL of each st around (28 sts).
Round 6: 1 dc into each st around (28 sts).
Round 7: 12 dc, (dc2tog, 1 dc) three times, 7 dc (25 sts).
Round 8: 8 dc, (dc2tog, 1 dc) four times, 5 dc (21 sts).
Round 9: 7 dc, (dc2tog, 1 dc) three times, 5 dc (18 sts).
Round 10: (5 dc, 2 dc into next st) three times (21 sts).
Round 11: 1 dc into each st around (21 sts).
At end of round 11, switch to yarn A, leaving yarn B on outside of leg to work boot detail later (**14**).
Round 12: using yarn A, 1 dc TBL of each st around (21 sts).
Round 13: 16 dc (16 sts). Stop this round here, leaving 5 sts unworked. Cut yarn and stuff leg.

14

SECOND LEG

Rounds 1–12 (12 rounds): as first leg.
Round 13: 1 dc into each st around (21 dc).
Round 14: 6 dc (6 sts). Stop this round here, leaving 15 sts unworked.
Do not cut yarn after last round, it will be used to crochet the legs together and make the body.

BOOT DETAIL (work for both legs)

1. Turn leg. Using yarn B and working TFL of round 11, insert hook into last st of round and draw through yarn B (**15**). Work 1 sl st into each st to end of round (21 sts). Cut yarn and weave in end.
2. Using yarn B and working TFL of round 4, insert hook into last st of round and draw through yarn B (**16**). 1 sl st into each st to end of round (28 sts).
Cut yarn and weave in end (**17**).

15

16

17

BODY

Continuing with yarn A and starting with the second leg, 1 ch (**18**) and 1 dc to join it to the first leg (see page 18); that will be the first stitch of the body (**19**).

Round 1: 1 dc into each st of first leg, 1 dc TFL of ch, 1 dc into each st of second leg, 1 dc TBL of ch (44 sts).
Round 2: 1 dc into each st around (44 sts).
Round 3: (10 dc, 2 dc into next st) four times (48 sts).
Rounds 4–9 (6 rounds): 1 dc into each st around (48 sts).
At end of round 9, work another 11 dc and move marker (if using) to last st worked (new end of round). Switch to yarn B (**20**).
Start stuffing the body, then continue stuffing as you go.
Round 10: using yarn B, 1 sl st TBL of each st around (48 sts).
Round 11: 1 dc TBL of each st around (48 sts).
Round 12: 1 dc into each st around (48 sts).
At end of round 12, switch to yarn A and cut yarn B.
Round 13: 1 sl st TBL of each st around (48 sts).
Round 14: 1 dc TBL of each st around (48 sts).
Rounds 15–17 (3 rounds): 1 dc into each st around (48 sts).
Round 18: 4 dc, (dc2tog, 6 dc) three times, 20 dc (45 sts).
Rounds 19 and 20 (2 rounds): 1 dc into each st around (45 sts).
Round 21: 3 dc, (dc2tog, 5 dc) three times, 21 dc (42 sts).
Rounds 22 and 23 (2 rounds): 1 dc into each st around (42 sts).
Round 24: (5 dc, dc2tog) six times (36 sts).
Round 25: 1 dc into each st around (36 sts).
Round 26: (4 dc, dc2tog) six times (30 sts).
Cut yarn, leaving a long enough tail for making up.
Position the 5mm (¼in) safety eyes or buttons in the middle of the tummy, with the first between rounds 17 and 18 of the body and the second between rounds 21 and 22 (**21**).

BELT BUCKLE

Using yarn I, 5 ch. The belt buckle is worked in rows from the foundation ch. Starting chs do not count as sts.
Row 1: starting in second ch from hook, 4 dc (4 sts).
Row 2: 1 ch (does not count as st here and throughout), turn, 4 dc (4 sts).
When you have completed row 2, work 1 dc in each st around to form a border.
Cut yarn, leaving a long enough tail for making up, work an invisible join (see page 19) (**22**).

18

19

20

21

22

MAKING UP THE BODY

Sew the buckle to the centre of the belt. Using yarn A, embroider belt loops around the trousers (**23, 24 and 25**). Sew on the arms two rounds below the last round of the body (**26**).

Attach the head, sewing into the back loops of the last round of the body, adding a little more stuffing just before closing up.

23

24

25

26

SACK

BAG

The bag is worked in joined rounds. Starting chs do not count as sts.

Round 1: using yarn F, 2 ch, 14 tr into an adjustable ring, join with sl st into top of first st (14 sts).

Round 2: 2 ch, 2 tr into each st around, join with sl st into top of first st (28 sts).

Round 3: 2 ch, (1 tr, 2 tr into next st) fourteen times, join with sl st into top of first st (42 sts).

Rounds 4–11 (**8 rounds**)**:** 2 ch, 1 tr into each st around, join with sl st into top of first st (42 sts).

Round 12: 2 ch, (1 tr, 3 tr into next st) twenty-one times, join with sl st into top of first st (84 sts).

Round 13: 2 ch, 1 tr into each st around, join with sl st into top of first st (84 sts).

Cut yarn, work an invisible join (see page 19) and weave in end (**27**).

CORD

Using yarn D, 101 ch. Starting in second ch from hook, 1 sl st into each st to end (100 sts).

Cut yarn and weave in end (**27**).

Thread the cord between the stitches of round 11 of the sack (**28 and 29**).

Put the little presents into the sack and tie a knot in the cord (**30 and 31**).

Instructions for the little crocheted presents can be found on pages 40–42.

27

28

29

30

31

ANNA *the little girl*

DIFFICULTY
***

Size: 22cm (9in)

What you need

- Basic kit (see pages 8–9)
- 2.25mm (UK 13, US 1) crochet hook
- 2 safety eyes, 6mm (¼in)
- 2 beads, 5mm (¼in)
- Pompom maker, 3.5cm (1½in)
- Black embroidery thread

Yarns (see pages 6 and 7 for substitution information)

- DMC Natura Just Cotton
  - 1 ball each in beige N81 (A), red N555 (B), white N01 (C), black N11 (D) and brown N41 (E)
- DMC Woolly
  - 1 ball in red 052 (F)
- DMC Woolly Chic
  - 1 ball in white 01 (G)
- DMC Teddy
  - 1 ball in white 310 (H)
- DMC Lumina
  - small amount in L3821 (I)

Anna is an adorable little girl. Like so many children, she absolutely loves Christmas and believes in magic. She loves preparing for the festivities with her little cat, Chi; together they decorate the house and make snowmen in the garden. Everything is buzzing before the big day. On Christmas Eve, before Anna goes to bed, she gets a piece of cake and a hot drink ready to leave out for Santa Claus.

LEG (make 2)

FIRST LEG

Round 1: using yarn E, 8 dc into an adjustable ring (8 sts).
Round 2: (2 dc into next st) eight times (16 sts).
Round 3: 1 dc, 2 dc into next st, 4 dc, (2 dc into next st) four times, 4 dc, 2 dc into next st, 1 dc (22 sts).
Round 4: 1 dc TBL of each st (22 sts).
Rounds 5 and 6 (2 rounds): 1 dc into each st around (22 sts).
Start stuffing the leg, then continue stuffing as you go.
Round 7: 7 dc, dc2tog four times, 7 dc (18 sts).
Round 8: 4 dc, (dc2tog, 2 dc) three times, 2 dc (15 sts).
At end of round 8, switch to yarn C. Leave yarn E outside the leg to work the boot detail later (**1**).
Round 9: using yarn C, (1 dc, 1 dec) TBL five times (10 sts).

1

Rounds 10–25 (16 rounds): 1 dc into each st around (10 sts).
Cut the yarn.
See box on next page for boot detail.

SECOND LEG

Rounds 1–25 (25 rounds): as first leg.
Round 26: 6 dc (6 sts). Stop this round here, leaving 4 sts unworked.
Do not cut yarn after last round; it will be used to crochet the legs together and make the body.

BOOT DETAIL (work for both legs)

1. Using yarn E and working TFL of round 8, insert hook into first st of round and draw through yarn E (**2**).

Round 1: (4 dc, 2 dc into next st) three times (18 dc).

Rounds 2–8 (7 rounds): 1 dc into each st around (18 dc).

Cut yarn, work an invisible join (see page 19) and weave in end.

2. Turn leg. Using yarn I and working TFL of round 3, insert hook into last st of round and draw through yarn I (3), 1 sl st into each st to end of round (22 sts).

Cut yarn and, using yarn I, embroider little laces (**4**).

Weave in end. You can roll down the boots (**5**).

2

3

4

5

6

7

BODY

Continuing with yarn C and starting with the second leg, 4 ch (**6**) and 1 dc to join it to the first leg (see page 18); this will be the first stitch of the body (**7**).

Round 1: 1 dc into each st of first leg, 4 dc TFL each of 4 ch, 1 dc into each st of second leg, 4 dc TBL of ch (28 sts).

Round 2: 2 dc, 2 dc into next st, 4 dc, (2 dc into next st. 2 dc) four times, (2 dc, 2 dc into next st) three times (36 sts).

Rounds 3–7 (5 rounds): 1 dc into each st around (36 sts).

At end of round 7, switch to yarn B and cut yarn C.

Start stuffing the body, then continue stuffing as you go.

Rounds 8 and 9: using yarn B, 1 dc TBL of each st around (36 sts).

Rounds 10 and 11 (2 rounds): 1 dc into each st around (36 sts).

Round 12: (7 dc, dc2tog) four times (32 sts).

Rounds 13–15 (3 rounds): 1 dc into each st around (32 sts).

Round 16: (6 dc, dc2tog) four times (28 sts).

Round 17: 1 dc into each st around (28 sts).

Round 18: (2 dc, dc2tog) seven times (21 sts).

At end of round 18, switch to yarn A and cut yarn B.

Round 19: using yarn A, (5 dc, dc2tog) TBL three times (18 sts).

Round 20: 1 dc into each st around (18 sts).

Cut yarn.

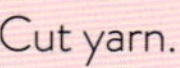

COLLAR

With the front of the body face up, mark the stitch at front centre with a pin (**8**). Turn body. Using yarn B and working TFL of round 18, insert hook into st next to pin and draw through yarn B (**9**). The collar is worked in rows. Starting chs do not count as sts.

Row 1: 2 ch, (2 tr, 2 tr into next st) six times, 3 tr (27 sts).

Row 2: 1 ch, turn, (3 dc, 2 dc into next st) six times, 3 dc (33 sts).

At end of round 2, switch to yarn H and cut yarn B.

Row 3: using yarn H, 1 ch, turn, 1 dc into each st to end (33 sts).

Cut yarn and weave in ends (**10**).

DRESS

SKIRT

Round 1: turn body. Using yarn B and working TFL of round 8, insert hook into last st of round and draw through yarn B (**11**), 1 ch, 2 dc into each st around (72 sts).

Rounds 2–15 (14 rounds): 1 dc into each st around (72 sts).

Cut yarn, work an invisible join (see page 19) then weave in end.

PETTICOAT

Turn body. Using yarn G and working TFL of round 7, insert hook into last st of round and draw through yarn G (**12**). The stitches will be worked in joined rounds. The petticoat is worked in joined rounds. Starting chs do not count as sts.

Rounds 1 and 2 (2 rounds): 2 ch, 1 tr into each st around, join with sl st into top of first st (36 sts).

Round 3: 2 ch, (1 tr, 2 tr into next st) eighteen times, join with sl st into top of first st (54 sts).

Rounds 4 and 5 (2 rounds): 2 ch, 1 tr into each st around, join with sl st into top of first st (54 sts).

Round 6: 1 ch, (2 dc, 2 dc into next st) 18 times, join with sl st into top of first st (72 sts).

Round 7: (4 ch, 1 sl st into next st) 72 times (360 sts).

Cut yarn and weave in end.

Sew two little beads onto the body for buttons (**13**).

8

10

12

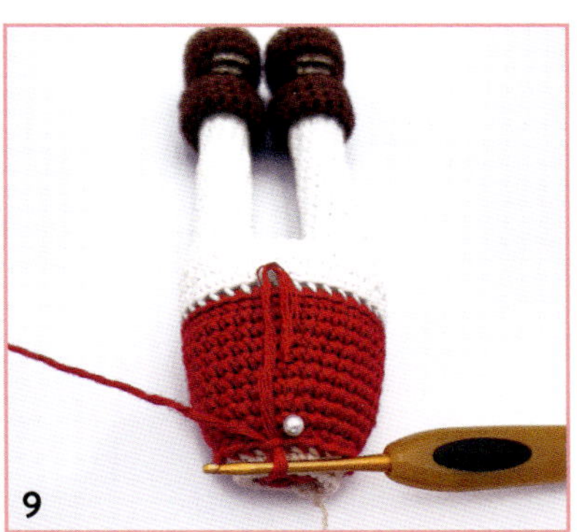
9

11

13

ARM (make 2)

Round 1: using yarn A, 8 dc into an adjustable ring (8 sts).
Round 2: (2 dc into next st, 3 dc) twice (10 sts).
Rounds 3–5 (3 rounds): 1 dc into each st around (10 sts).
At end of round 5, switch to yarn B and cut yarn A.
Round 6: (4 dc, 2 dc into next st) twice (12 sts).
Round 7: 1 dc TBL of each st (12 sts).
Rounds 8–14 (7 rounds): 1 dc into each st around (12 sts).
Fold the arm flat and line up the stitches on both sides of the opening (**14**). Work 1 dc in each pair of sts opposite each other along the top to close (6 sts).
Cut yarn, leaving a long enough tail for making up.

HEAD

Round 1: using yarn A, 8 dc into an adjustable ring (8 sts).
Round 2: (2 dc into next st) eight times (16 sts).
Round 3: (1 dc, 2 dc into next st) eight times (24 sts).
Round 4: (2 dc, 2 dc into next st) eight times (32 sts).
Round 5: (3 dc, 2 dc into next st) eight times (40 sts).
Round 6: 1 dc into each st around (40 sts).
Round 7: (4 dc, 2 dc into next st) eight times (48 sts).

SLEEVE DETAIL (work for both arms)

Turn arm. Using yarn B and working TFL of round 6, insert hook into last st of round and draw through yarn B (15), 1 ch, 1 htr into each st around, join with sl st into top of first st (12 sts).
Cut yarn and weave in end (16).

15

16

Rounds 8–11 (4 rounds): 1 dc into each st around (48 sts).
Round 12: 24 dc, (dc2tog, 4 dc) four times (44 sts).
Rounds 13–15 (3 rounds): 1 dc into each st around (44 sts).
Round 16: 21 dc, (2 dc into next st, 2 dc) three times, 5 dc, (2 dc into next st, 2 dc) three times (50 sts).
Rounds 17–20 (4 rounds): 1 dc into each st around (50 sts).
Place the eyes between rounds 15 and 16, with the first eye between sts 27 and 28 of round 15 and the second between sts 35 and 36.
Start stuffing the head, then continue stuffing as you go.
Round 21: (8 dc, dc2tog) five times (45 sts).
Round 22: 3 dc, dc2tog, (7 dc, dc2tog) four times, 4 dc (40 sts).
Round 23: (6 dc, dc2tog) five times (35 sts).
Round 24: 2 dc, dc2tog, (5 dc, dc2tog) four times, 3 dc (30 sts).
Round 25: (3 dc, dc2tog) six times (24 sts).
Round 26: 1 dc,dc2tog, (2 dc, dc2tog) five times, 1 dc (18 sts).
Cut yarn, leaving a long enough tail for making up.
Using black embroidery thread, embroider eyebrows 2 rounds above each eye.
Using yarn A, embroider a nose between the eyes on round 16. Apply pink blusher to the cheeks (17).

14

17

HAIR

Round 1: using yarn D, 8 dc into adjustable ring (8 sts).
Round 2: (2 dc into next st) eight times (16 sts).
Round 3: (1 dc, 2 dc into next st) eight times (24 sts).
Round 4: first layer of hair, working TBL, *40 ch (**18**). Starting in second ch from hook, 39 dc, miss 1 st, 1 sl st into next st (**19**); rep from * to * six times. Six long strands made.
30 ch. Starting in second ch from hook, 29 dc, miss 1 st, 1 sl st into next st. One mid-length strand made.
20 ch. Starting in second ch from hook, 19 dc, miss 1 st, 1 sl st into next st. One mid-length strand made.
12 ch. Starting in second ch from hook, 11 dc, miss 1 st, 1 sl st into next st; rep from * to * twice. Two short strands made.
20 ch. Starting in second ch from hook, 19 dc; miss 1 st; 1 sl st into next st. One mid-length strand made.
30 ch. Starting in second ch from hook, 29 dc, miss 1 st, 1 sl st into next st. One mid-length strand made.
12 strands made in total.
Second layer of hair: work TFL of round 3, 1 sl st into first st (**20**), then work as for first layer of hair.
Cut yarn, leaving a long enough tail for making up (**21**).

18

19

20

21

EAR (make 2)

Using yarn A, work 2 ch, 4 tr, 2 ch, 1 sl st into an adjustable ring. Pull to close ring. Cut yarn, leaving a long enough tail for making up (**22**).

22

HAT

Using yarn F, 4 ch. The brim is worked in rows from this foundation ch. Starting chs do not count as sts.

Row 1: starting in second ch from hook, 3 dc (3 sts).

Row 2: 1 ch (does not count as st here and throughout), turn, 3 dc (3 sts).

Row 3: 1 ch, turn, 3 dc TBL (3 sts).

Rows 4–59 (56 rows): rep rounds 2 and 3 twenty-eight more times.

Row 60: 1 ch, turn, 3 dc (3 sts).

At end of row 60 (**23**), join with sl st to row 1 to close the brim (**24**). Do not cut yarn.

The hat is worked in joined rounds around the brim. Starting chs do not count as sts.

Round 1: continuing with yarn F, 1 ch, (3 dc, 2 dc into next st) fifteen times, join with sl st into top of first st (75 sts).

Round 2: 2 ch, 1 tr into each st around, join with sl st into top of first st (75 sts).

Round 3: 1 ch, (13 dc, dc2tog) five times, join with sl st into top of first st (70 sts).

Round 4: 2 ch, 1 tr into each st around, join with sl st into top of first st (70 sts).

Round 5: 1 ch, (5 dc, dc2tog) ten times, join with sl st into top of first st (60 sts).

Round 6: 2 ch, 1 tr into each st around, join with sl st into top of first st (60 sts).

Round 7: 1 ch, (4 dc, dc2tog) ten times, join with sl st into top of first st (50 sts).

Round 8: 2 ch, 1 tr into each st around, join with sl st into top of first st (50 sts).

23

24

25

Round 9: 1 ch (8 dc, dc2tog) five times, join with sl st into top of first st (45 sts).
Round 10: 2 ch, 1 tr into each st around, join with sl st into top of first st (45 sts).
Cut yarn, leaving a long enough tail for making up.
Sew up rows 1 and 60 to join the brim of the hat (**25 and 26**).
Sew round 10 of the hat closed with a few stitches (**27 and 28**).
Using a pompom maker and yarn G, make a 3.5cm (1½in) pompom then sew onto the hat.
Using yarn I, embroider little hearts on the hat (**29**).

26

28

27

29

MAKING UP

Use pins to hold the ears in place on either side of the head at rounds 15 and 17, approximately 6 sts from the eyes, then sew (**30 and 31**).

Place the hair on the head, right side out (**32**). Pin the strands in place (**33**) then sew them onto the head, taking care not to sew down the eight strands over the forehead (**34**).

Sew on the arms 1 round below the neck (**35**).

Attach the head, adding a little more stuffing just before closing up.

Sew the hat onto the head.

32

33

30

34

31

35

CHI THE KITTEN *and the stockings*

DIFFICULTY
***

Size: 7cm (2¾in)

What you need

- Basic kit (see pages 8–9)
- 2.25mm (UK 13, US 1) crochet hook (main hook – use this hook unless stated otherwise)
- 2.75mm (UK 12, US 2) crochet hook (for the stocking)
- 2 safety eyes, 6mm (¼in)
- Brown embroidery thread

Yarns (see pages 6 and 7 for substitution information)

- DMC Natura Just Cotton
  - 1 ball in yellow N83 (A)
  - small amounts in red N555 (B) and brown N41 (C)
- DMC Woolly
  - 1 ball each in mustard 959 (D), red 052 (E) and green 086 (F)
- DMC Teddy
  - 1 ball in white 310 (G)
- DMC Lumina
  - 1 ball in L3821 (H)
- DMC Woolly Chic (for alternative stocking colourway)
  - small amount in white 01 (I)

Chi the kitten is hilarious. Once everyone is asleep, he sneaks into a stocking hanging from the chimney because he plans to hide there and surprise Santa Claus. The stocking is so soft and the chimney breast so warm and comfortable, let's see whether Chi can manage to keep his eyes open (I think he'll find it difficult!).

HEAD AND BODY

Round 1: using yarn A, 7 dc into an adjustable ring (7 sts).
Round 2: (2 dc into next st) seven times (14 sts).
Round 3: (1 dc, 2 dc into next st) seven times (21 sts).
Round 4: 2 dc, 2 dc into next st, (using yarn A, 2 dc, using yarn D, 2 dc into next st) three times, using yarn A, (2 dc, 2 dc into next st) three times (28 sts).
Round 5: 1 dc, 2 dc into next st, 2 dc, (using yarn A, 1 dc, 2 dc into next st, using yarn D, 2 dc) three times, using yarn A, 1 dc, (2 dc into next st, 3 dc) twice, 2 dc into next st, 2 dc (35 sts).
Round 6: 2 dc, 2 dc into next st, 4 dc, 2 dc into next st, (using yarn D, 2 dc, using yarn A, 3 dc) twice, using yarn D, 2 dc, using yarn A, 2 dc into next st, 4 dc, 2 dc into next st, 5 dc, 2 dc into next st, 3 dc (40 sts).
Round 7: 10 dc, (using yarn D, 2 dc, using yarn A, 3 dc) three times, using yarn A, 15 dc (40 sts).
Round 8: 11 dc, using yarn D, 1 dc, using yarn A, 3 dc, using yarn D, 2 dc, using yarn A, 3 dc, using yarn D, 1 dc, using yarn A, 19 dc (40 sts).

Round 9: 16 dc, using yarn D, 1 dc, using yarn A, 23 dc (40 sts).
Cut yarn D and continue with yarn A.
Rounds 10 and 11 (2 rounds): 1 dc into each st around (40 sts).
Round 12: (7 dc, 2 dc into next st) five times (45 sts).
Rounds 13–15 (3 rounds): 1 dc into each st around (45 sts).
Place the eyes between rounds 11 and 12, 5 sts apart (the lines worked in yarn D should be in the middle of the head).
Start stuffing the head, then continue stuffing as you go.
Round 16: (7 dc, dc2tog) five times (40 sts).
Round 17: (3 dc, dc2tog) eight times (32 sts).
Round 18: 1 dc, dc2tog, (2 dc, dc2tog) seven times, 1 dc (24 sts).
Round 19: (2 dc, dc2tog) six times (18 sts).
Round 20: 1 sl st into each st around (18 sts).
Round 21: (2 dc, 2 dc into next st) six times (24 sts).
Round 22: 1 dc, 2 dc into next st, (3 dc, 2 dc into next st) five times, 2 dc (30 sts).
Round 23: 21 dc, using yarn D, 9 dc (30 sts).
Round 24: 9 dc, using yarn A, 21 dc (30 sts).
Round 25: 1 dc into each st around (30 sts).
Round 26: (4 dc, 2 dc into next st) four times, using yarn D, (4 dc, 2 dc into next st) twice (36 sts).
Round 27: 11 dc, using yarn A, 25 dc (36 sts).
Round 28: 1 dc into each st around (36 sts).
Round 29: 25 dc, using yarn D, 11 dc (36 sts).
Round 30: 10 dc, using yarn A, 26 dc (36 sts).
Cut yarn D and continue with yarn A.
Round 31: (7 dc, dc2tog) four times (32 sts).
Round 32: (2 dc, dc2tog) eight times (24 sts).
Round 33: (dc2tog, 1 dc) eight times (16 sts).
Round 34: dc2tog eight times (8 sts).
Finish stuffing the body. Fasten off and tie off remaining sts.
Using embroidery thread, embroider a nose between the eyes, over round 13 and whiskers under each eye (**1**).

ARM (make 2)

Round 1: using yarn A, 8 dc into an adjustable ring (8 sts).
Round 2: (2 dc into next st, 3 dc) twice (10 sts).
Rounds 3–6 (4 rounds): 1 dc into each st around (10 sts).
Fold the arm flat and line up the stitches on both sides of the opening (**2**). Work 1 dc in each pair of sts opposite each other along the top to close (5 sts).
Cut yarn, leaving a long enough tail for making up.
Using the embroidery thread, embroider claws over round 2 (**3**).

1

LEG (make 2)

Round 1: using yarn A, 8 dc into an adjustable ring (8 sts).
Round 2: (2 dc into next st, 1 dc) four times (12 sts).
Rounds 3–6 (4 rounds): 1 dc into each st around (12 sts).
Fold the leg flat and line up the stitches on both sides of the opening. Work 1 dc in each pair of sts opposite each other along the top to close (6 sts).
Cut yarn, leaving a long enough tail for making up.
Using embroidery thread, embroider claws over round 2 (**3**).

EAR (make 2)

Round 1: using yarn A, 6 dc into an adjustable ring (6 sts).
Round 2: (2 dc into next st, 2 dc) twice (8 sts).
Round 3: (2 dc into next st, 3 dc) twice (10 sts).
Round 4: (2 dc into next st, 4 dc) twice (12 sts).
Round 5: (2 dc, 2 dc into next st) four times (16 sts).
Round 6: 1 dc into each st around (16 sts).
Cut yarn, leaving a long enough tail for making up (**4**).

TAIL

Round 1: using yarn D, 6 dc into an adjustable ring (6 sts).
Round 2: (2 dc into next st, 1 dc) three times (9 sts).
Round 3: 1 dc into each st around (9 sts).
Rounds 4–6 (3 rounds): dc2tog, 3 dc, 2 dc into next st, 3 dc (9 sts).
At end of round 6, switch to yarn A and cut yarn D.
Start stuffing the tail, then continue stuffing as you go.
Rounds 7 and 8 (2 rounds): using yarn A, dc2tog, 3 dc, 2 dc into next st, 3 dc (9 sts).
Rounds 9–23 (15 rounds): 1 dc into each st around (9 sts).
Fold the tail flat and line up the stitches on both sides of the opening. Work 1 dc in each pair of sts opposite each other along the top to close (4 sts).
Cut yarn, leaving a long enough tail for making up (**4**).

2

3

4

CAPE

Using yarn B, 26 ch. The cape is worked in rows from this foundation ch. Starting chs do not count as sts.
Row 1: starting in third ch from hook, 24 htr (24 sts).
Row 2: 1 ch, turn, (3 dc, 2 dc into next st) six times (30 sts).
Row 3: turn, (2 ch, 1 sl st into next st) thirty times (90 sts).
Cut yarn and weave in end.

TIE

Using yarn B, 8 ch, then 1 dc into each st along the foundation ch (**5**), 12 ch. Cut yarn (**6**).

HEADBAND

The headband is made up of antlers and a band.

ANTLER (make 2)

The antlers are made of two small pieces that will be joined together. Stuff as you go.

PIECE ONE

Round 1: using yarn C, 6 dc into an adjustable ring (6 sts).
Rounds 2–4 (3 rounds): 1 dc into each st around (6 sts).
Cut yarn.

PIECE TWO

Round 1: using yarn C, 6 dc into an adjustable ring (6 sts).
Rounds 2 and 3 (2 rounds): 1 dc into each st around (6 sts).
Do not cut yarn. Join to first piece with 1 sl st (see page 18), which will be first st of next round (**7**).
Round 4: 1 dc into each st of first piece, 1 dc into each st of second piece (12 sts).
Round 5: dc2tog six times (6 sts).
Round 6: 1 dc into each st around (6 sts).
Cut yarn, leaving a long enough tail for making up (**8**).

BAND

Using yarn H, 20 ch. Starting in second ch from hook, 18 dc TFL, 3 dc into last st. Continuing on other side, 17 dc TBL of ch, 2 dc into next st, join with sl st into top of first st (40 sts).
Cut yarn, leaving a long enough tail for making up (**8**).

5

7

6

8

MAKING UP

Pin the ears in place on either side of the head on rounds 3 and 10 (**9**), then sew on. Pin the arms and legs to either side of the body (**10**), then sew on.
Sew the tail to the middle of the back (**11 and 12**).
Apply pink blusher to the cheeks and inside the ears.
Pin the head band in place on the head (**13**), then sew on.
Sew the antlers to the head band.
Place the cape around the kitten's shoulders (**14**).

9

12

10

13

11

14

STOCKING

The stocking is worked using yarns E, F and G.
Round 1: using yarn E and 2.75mm (UK 12, US 2) crochet hook, 6 dc into an adjustable ring (6 sts).
Round 2: (2 dc into next st) six times (12 sts).
Round 3: (1 dc, 2 dc into next st) six times (18 sts).
Round 4: (2 dc, 2 dc into next st) six times (24 sts).
Round 5: 1 dc, 2 dc into next st, (3 dc, 2 dc into next st) five times, 2 dc (30 sts).
At end of round 5, switch to yarn F. Do not cut yarn E.
Round 6: (4 dc, 2 dc into next st) six times (36 sts).
Rounds 7–10 (4 rounds): 1 dc into each st around (36 sts).
Round 11: using yarn E, 1 dc into each st around (36 sts).
Round 12: using yarn F, 1 dc into each st around (36 sts).
Round 13: using yarn F, 2 dc, (using yarn E, 1 dc, using yarn F, 3 dc) eight times, using yarn E, 1 dc, using yarn F, 1 dc (36 sts).
Round 14: using yarn F, 1 dc into each st around (36 sts).
Round 15: using yarn E, 1 dc into each st around (36 sts).
At end of round 15, switch to yarn F and cut yarn E.
Rounds 16 and 17 (2 rounds): 1 dc into each st around (36 sts).
Round 18: 28 dc (28 sts) Fasten off this round here. Switch to yarn E. Do not cut yarn F, to continue working leg of stocking later.
Next work heel of stocking in rows. Starting chs do not count as sts.
Row 1: continuing with yarn E, 16 dc (16 sts).
Row 2: 1 ch, turn, 16 dc (16 sts).
Row 3: 1 ch, turn, 7 dc, dc2tog, 7 dc (15 sts).
Row 4: 1 ch, turn. 7 dc, dc2tog, 6 dc (14 sts).
Row 5: 1 ch, turn, 6 dc, dc2tog, 6 dc (13 sts).
Row 6: 1 ch, turn, 6 dc, dc2tog, 5 dc (12 sts).
Row 7: 1 ch, turn, 5 dc, dc2tog, 5 dc (11 sts).
Row 8: 1 ch, turn, 5 dc, dc2tog, 4 dc (10 sts).
Cut yarn, leaving a long enough tail for making up (**15**).
Fold last row of heel in half, pinch both sides together and sew up (**16 and 17**).

15

16

17

Continue working around heel and into remaining sts of round 18. Using yarn F, insert hook into first st of heel (where you fastened off round 18) and draw through yarn (**18**), forming first st of next round.

Round 19: 1 ch, 16 dc into heel, 20 dc into remaining sts of round 18 (36 sts).

Rounds 20–23 (4 rounds): 1 dc into each st around (36 sts). At end of round 23, work another 8 dc and move marker (if using) to last st worked (new end of round).

Round 24: (using yarn E, 1 dc, using yarn F, 3 dc) eight times, using yarn E, 1 dc, using yarn F, 2 dc, using yarn E, 1 dc (36 sts).

Round 25: using yarn E, 2 dc (using yarn F, 1 dc, using yarn E, 3 dc) eight times, using yarn F, 2 dc (36 sts).

Cut yarn E and continue with yarn F.

Rounds 26–28 (3 rounds): 1 dc into each st around (36 sts). At end of round 28, switch to yarn G and cut yarn F.

Round 29: 1 ch, 36 tr, join with sl st into top of first st (36 sts). Cut yarn and weave in ends.

Using yarn H, embroider stocking detail (see page 23) (**19**).

18

19

HANGING LOOP

Long version: using yarn F, 60 ch. Cut yarn and sew to either side of the stocking at round 28 (**20 and 21**).
Short version: using yarn F, 25 ch. Cut yarn and sew to either side of stocking at round 28 (**22 and 23**).
The white stocking is crocheted using yarn I and yarn E.
The red stocking is crocheted using yarns E and F; you simply need to reverse the colours.

21

22

20

23

CARO AND TOMA *the snowmen*

DIFFICULTY
**

Size: 16cm (6½in)

What you need

- Basic kit (see pages 8–9)
- 4mm (UK 8, US 6), 2.25mm (UK 13, US 1) and 2.5mm (UK 12/13, US 1/2) crochet hooks
- 2 safety eyes, 8mm (¼in)
- 2 buttons, 11mm (½in)
- Black embroidery thread
- Yellow embroidery thread

Yarns (see pages 6 and 7 for substitution information)

- DMC Natura Just Cotton
  - 1 ball each in brown N41 (A) and orange N105 (B)
- DMC Woolly
  - 1 ball each in green 082 (C), dark green 086 (D), yellow 959 (E) and red 052 (F)
- DMC Velvet
  - 1 ball in white 002 (G)
- DMC Teddy
  - 1 ball in white 310 (H)
- DMC Lumina
  - small amount in L3821 (I)

Caro and Toma are the snowmen that Anna has made in her garden after a heavy fall of snow. They are still there, in this peaceful spot, enjoying each winter day, especially when the sun shines on them. They think that summer must be lovely, but they can only imagine what it must be like.

LARGE SNOWMAN – HEAD AND BODY

Round 1: using yarn G and 4mm (UK 8, US 6) crochet hook, 7 dc into an adjustable ring (7 sts).
Round 2: (2 dc into next st) seven times (14 sts).
Round 3: (1 dc, 2 dc into next st) seven times (21 sts).
Round 4: (2 dc, 2 dc into next st) seven times (28 sts).
Rounds 5–9 (5 rounds): 1 dc into each st around (28 sts).
Round 10: (dc2tog, 2 dc) seven times (21 sts).
Attach eyes between rounds 6 and 7, 2 sts apart.
Start stuffing the head, then continue stuffing as you go.
Round 11: (5 dc, dc2tog) three times (18 sts).
Round 12: 1 sl st into each st around (18 sts).
Round 13: (2 dc, 2 dc into next st) six times (24 sts).
Round 14: (3 dc, 2 dc into next st) six times (30 sts).
Rounds 15–17 (3 rounds): 1 dc into each st around (30 sts).
Round 18: (14 dc, 2 dc into next st) twice (32 sts).
Rounds 19 and 20 (2 rounds): 1 dc into each st around (32 sts).
Round 21: (dc2tog, 2 dc) eight times (24 sts).
Round 22: (1 dc, dc2tog) eight times (16 sts).
Round 23: dc2tog eight times (8 sts).
Finish stuffing the body. Fasten off and tie off remaining sts (**1**).

1

2

3

4

5

6

7

8

9

NOSE

Round 1: using yarn B and 2.25mm (UK 13, US 1) crochet hook, 6 dc into an adjustable ring (6 sts).
Round 2: (2 dc into next st, 2 dc) twice (8 sts).
Round 3: (3 dc, 2 dc into next st) twice (10 sts).
Round 4: 1 dc into each st around (10 sts).
Round 5: (4 dc, 2 dc into next st) twice (12 sts).
Rounds 6 and 7 (2 rounds): 1 dc into each st around (12 sts).
Round 8: (5 dc, 2 dc into next st) twice (14 sts).
Rounds 9 and 10 (2 rounds): 1 dc into each st around (14 sts).
Cut yarn, leaving a long enough tail for making up.
Stuff the nose. Using yellow embroidery thread, embroider little marks to make it look like a carrot (**2**).
Sew the nose onto the head. Using brown embroidery thread, embroider the mouth below the nose (**3 and 4**).

ARM (make 2)

The arms are made of two small pieces (**5**) that will be joined together.
Stuff as you go.

PIECE ONE

Round 1: using yarn A and 2.25mm (UK 13, US 1) crochet hook, 7 dc into an adjustable ring (7 sts).
Round 2: 1 dc TBL of each st around (7 sts).
Round 3: 1 dc into each st around (7 sts).
Cut the yarn.

PIECE TWO

Round 1: using yarn A and 2.25mm (UK 13, US 1) crochet hook, 8 dc into an adjustable ring (8 sts).
Round 2: 1 dc TBL of each st around (8 sts).
Rounds 3–6 (4 rounds): 1 dc into each st around (8 sts).
Do not cut yarn. Join to first piece with 1 sl st (see page 18), which will be first st of next round (**6**).
Round 7: 1 dc into each st of first section, 1 dc into each st of second section (15 sts).
Round 8: dc2tog seven times, 1 dc (8 sts).
Rounds 9–14 (6 rounds): 1 dc into each st around (8 sts).
Cut yarn, leaving a long enough tail for making up (**7**).
Sew the arms to the body; there is no need to make them symmetrical. Sew the buttons to the tummy (**8**).

SCARF

Using yarn F and 2.25mm (UK 13, US 1) crochet hook, 135 ch. Starting in second ch from hook, 1 dc TFL into each of next 133 sts, 3 dc into last st. Continuing on other side, 1 dc TFL into each of next 132 sts, 2 dc into last st, join with sl st into top of first st (270 sts). Cut yarn and weave in end (**9**).

EARMUFFS

The earmuffs consist of two half-spheres and a headband.

HALF-SPHERE (MAKE 2)

Each half-sphere consists of an inner piece and an outer piece.

OUTER PIECE

Round 1: using yarn D and 2.25mm (UK 13, US 1) crochet hook, 6 dc into adjustable ring (6 sts).
Round 2: (2 dc into next st) six times (12 sts).
Round 3: (1 dc, 2 dc into next st) six times (18 sts).
Round 4: (2 dc, 2 dc into next st) six times (24 sts).
Round 5: 1 dc into each st around (24 sts).
Cut the yarn.

INNER PIECE

Round 1: using yarn C and 2.25mm (UK 13, US 1) crochet hook, 8 dc into an adjustable ring (8 sts).
Round 2: (2 dc into next st) eight times (16 sts).
Round 3: (1 dc, 2 dc into next st) eight times (24 sts).
Do not cut yarn after last round; it will be used to sew the two pieces together to form the half-sphere (**10**).
Round 4: place inside and outside pieces wrong sides together and crochet together round 5 of outer piece (yarn D) and round 3 of inner piece (yarn C) (**11**). Stuff half-sphere and close up by working 1 ch, 1 dc into each st around, join with sl st into top of first st.
Cut yarn (**12**).

HEADBAND

Using yarn C and 2.25mm (UK 13, US 1) crochet hook, 55 ch. Starting in second ch from hook, 2 dc TFL into same st, 1 dc TFL into each of next 52 sts, 4 dc TFL into last st. Continuing on other side, 1 dc TBL of each of next 52 sts, 2 dc into last st, join with sl st into top of first st (112 sts).

Cut yarn, leaving a long enough tail for making up.
Fold the piece in half and sew along the full length (**13 and 14**).
Sew the half-spheres to each end of the headband (**15 and 16**). Sew the earmuffs to the head.
Arrange the scarf around the neck.

SMALL SNOWMAN – HEAD AND BODY

Round 1: using yarn G and 4mm (UK 8, US 6) crochet hook, 6 dc into an adjustable ring (6 sts).
Round 2: (2 dc into next st) six times (12 sts).
Round 3: (1 dc, 2 dc into next st) six times (18 sts).
Round 4: (2 dc, 2 dc into next st) six times (24 sts).
Rounds 5–8 (4 rounds): 1 dc into each st around (24 sts).
Start stuffing the head, then continue stuffing as you go.

Round 9: (dc2tog, 1 dc) eight times (16 sts).
Round 10: 1 sl st into each st around (16 sts).
Round 11: (3 dc, 2 dc into next st) four times (20 sts).
Round 12: (3 dc, 2 dc into next st) five times (25 sts).
Rounds 13–16 (4 rounds): 1 dc into each st around (25 sts).
Round 17: dc2tog, 23 dc (24 sts).
Round 18: (dc2tog, 1 dc) eight times (16 sts).

Round 19: dc2tog eight times (8 sts).
Finish stuffing the body. Fasten off and tie off remaining sts.
Using black embroidery thread, embroider eyes over round 6, 3 sts apart (**17**).

18

19

20

NOSE

Round 1: using yarn F and 2.25mm (UK 13, US 1) crochet hook, 7 dc into an adjustable ring (7 sts).
Round 2: 1 dc into each st around (7 sts).
Cut yarn, leaving a long enough tail for making up.
Sew the nose to the head.
Using yarn A, embroider the mouth below the nose (**18**).

ARM (make 2)

Stuff as you go.
Round 1: using yarn A and 2.25mm (UK 13, US 1) crochet hook, 8 dc into an adjustable ring (8 sts).
Round 2: 1 dc TBL of each st (8 sts).
Rounds 3–9 (7 rounds): 1 dc into each st around (8 sts).
Cut yarn, leaving a long enough tail for making up.

LITTLE LEAF (make 2)

Using yarn C and 2.25mm (UK 13, US 1) crochet hook, 5 ch. Starting in second ch from hook, 1 sl st, 1 dc, 1 htr, 1 sl st (4 sts).
Cut yarn, leaving a long enough tail for making up.
Sew the leaves to the arms (**19**).
Sew the arms to the body; there is no need to make them symmetrical.
Using yarn I, embroider two lines on the tummy for buttons (**20**).

HAT

Using yarn E and 2.5mm (UK 12/13, US 1/2) crochet hook, 48 ch and join with sl st into first st (**21**). The hat is worked in joined rounds. Starting chs do not count as sts.
Round 1: 2 ch, 1 tr into st around, join with sl st into top of first st (48 sts).
Round 2: 1 ch (10 dc, dc2tog) four times, join with sl st into top of first st (44 sts).
Round 3: 2 ch, 1 tr into each st around, join with sl st into top of first st (44 sts).
Round 4: 1 ch, 1 dc into each around, join with sl st into top of first st (44 sts).
Round 5: 2 ch, 1 tr into each st, around, join with sl st into top of first st (44 sts).
Round 6: 1 ch, (9 dc, dc2tog) four times, join with sl st into top of first st (40 sts).
Round 7: 2 ch, 1 tr into each around, join with sl st into top of first st (40 sts).
Round 8: 1 ch, 1 dc into each around, join with sl st into top of first st (40 sts).
Round 9: 2 ch, 1 tr into each around, join with sl st into top of first st (40 sts).
Cut yarn, leaving a long enough tail for making up.
Sew up round 9 of the hat with a few stitches (**22 and 23**).

21

22

23

BRIM

Turn hat. Using yarn H and 2.5mm (UK 12/13, US 1/2) crochet hook and working into loops of round 1 foundation ch, insert hook into last st, draw through yarn H (**24**), 1 ch, 1 dc into each st around, join with sl st into top of first st (48 sts).
Cut yarn and weave in end.

POMPOM

Round 1: using yarn H and 2.5mm (UK 12/13, US 1/2) crochet hook, 6 dc into an adjustable ring (6 sts).
Round 2: (2 dc into next st) six times (12 sts).
Round 3: (2 dc into next st) six times, 1 dc) six times (18 sts).
Round 4: 1 dc into each st around (18 sts).
Stuff the pompom.
Round 5: (1 dc, dc2tog) six times (12 sts).
Round 6: dc2tog six times (6 sts).
Cut yarn, leaving a long enough tail for the seam and tie off remaining sts.
Using yarn I, embroider little hearts on the hat.
Sew the pompom to the top of the hat (**25**).

24

25

THE CHRISTMAS *Angel*

DIFFICULTY
**

Size: 20cm (8in)

What you need

- Basic kit (see pages 8–9)
- 2.25mm (UK 13, US 1) crochet hook (main hook – use unless stated otherwise)
- 2.75mm (UK 12, US 2) crochet hook (for the wings)
- Felting needle
- Wire
- Black embroidery thread
- Brown embroidery thread
- White embroidery thread

Yarns (see pages 6 and 7 for substitution information)

- DMC Natura Just Cotton
  - 1 ball each in beige N81 (A) and white N01 (B)
- DMC Woolly Chic
  - 1 ball in white 01 (C)
- DMC Big Knit
  - 1 ball in blue 106 (D)
- DMC Teddy
  - 1 ball in white 310 (E)
- DMC Lumina
  - small amount in L3821 (F)

On Christmas Eve, when all the world is asleep (I think that even includes Chi the kitten), a little angel is singing the most beautiful song and wishing for a peaceful world in which everyone will find love. Happy Christmas to one and all!

LEG (make 2)

Round 1: using yarn B, 8 dc into an adjustable ring (8 sts).
Round 2: (2 dc into next st, 1 dc) four times (12 sts).
Rounds 3–9 (7 rounds): 1 dc into each st around (12 sts).
At end of round 9, switch to yarn E and cut yarn B.
Start stuffing the leg, then continue stuffing as you go.
Rounds 10 and 11 (2 rounds): using yarn E, 1 dc into each st around (12 sts).
At end of round 11, switch to yarn A and cut yarn E.
Rounds 12–21 (10 rounds): using yarn A, 1 dc into each st around (12 sts).
Cut yarn at end of first leg.
At end of second leg, switch to yarn B (**1**), ready to join the legs and work body. Cut yarn A.

1

BODY

The body is worked from the joined legs. Continuing with yarn B and starting with the second leg, 3 ch (**2**) and 1 dc to join it to the first leg (see page 18); this will be the first stitch of the body (**3**).

Round 1: 1 dc into each st of first leg, 3 dc TFL of 3 ch, 1 dc into each st of second leg, 3 dc TBL of ch (30 sts).

Round 2: 13 dc, 2 dc into next st, 14 dc, 2 dc into next st 1 dc (32 sts).

Rounds 3–12 (10 rounds): 1 dc into each st around (32 sts).

Start stuffing the body, then continue stuffing as you go.

Round 13: (6 dc, dc2tog) four times (28 sts).

Rounds 14–16 (3 rounds): 1 dc into each st around (28 sts).

Round 17: (5 dc, dc2tog) four times (24 sts).

Round 18: 1 dc into each st around (24 sts).

At end of round 18, switch to yarn A and cut yarn B.

Round 19: using yarn A, (2 dc, 1 dec) TBL six times (18 sts).

Round 20: 1 dc into each st around (18 sts).

Cut the yarn.

DRESS

Turn body. Using yarn C and working TFL of round 18, insert hook into last st of round and draw through yarn C (**4**). The dress is worked in joined rounds. Starting chs do not count as sts.

Round 1: 1 ch, 1 dc into each st around, join with sl st into top of first st (24 sts).

Round 2: 2 ch, 1 tr TBL into each st, join with sl st (24 sts).

Round 3: 1 ch, (3 dc, 2 dc into next st) six times, join with sl st into top of first st (30 sts).

Round 4: 2 ch, 1 tr into each st, join with sl st into top of first st (30 sts).

Round 5: 1 ch, (4 dc, 2 dc into next st) six times, join with sl st into top of first st (36 sts).

Round 6: 2 ch, 1 tr into each st, join with sl st into top of first st (36 sts).

Round 7: 1 ch, (8 dc, 2 dc into next st) four times, join with sl st into top of first st (40 sts).

Rounds 8–11 (4 rounds): 2 ch, 1 tr into each st, join with sl st into top of first st (40 sts).

Round 12: 1 ch, (9 dc, 2 dc into next st) four times, join with sl st into top of first st (44 sts).

Round 13: (miss 1 st, 3 tr into next st, miss 1 st, 1 sl st) eleven times (44 sts).

Cut yarn and weave in end.

COLLAR

With the front of the body face up, mark the stitch at front centre with a pin. Turn body, body. Using yarn C and working TFL of round 1 of dress, insert hook into marked st and draw through yarn C (**5**). The collar is worked in rows. Starting chs do not count as sts.

Row 1: 2 ch, 1 htr, 2 htr into next st, (3 htr, 2 htr into next st) five times, 2 htr (30 sts).

Row 2: 2 ch, turn, 2 htr, 2 htr into next st, (4 htr, 2 htr into next st) five times, 2 htr (36 sts).

Row 3: 2 ch, turn, 1 htr into each st (36 sts).

Row 4: turn, (3 ch, 1 sl st into next st) thirty-six times (144 sts).

Cut yarn and weave in end.

Using yarn C, make two little pompoms, both around 8mm (¼in) diameter. Using yarn F, join the pompoms and sew the yarn to the dress (**6**).

2

3

4

5

6

ARM (make 2)

Round 1: using yarn A, 8 dc into an adjustable ring (8 sts).
Round 2: (2 dc into next st, 3 dc) twice (10 sts).
Rounds 3–16 (14 rounds): 1 dc into each st around (10 sts).
Fold the arm flat and line up the stitches on both sides of the opening (**7**). Work 1 dc in each pair of sts opposite each other along the top to close (5 sts).
Cut yarn, leaving a long enough tail for making up (**8**).

WING (make 2)

Round 1: using yarn E and 2.75mm (UK 12, US 2) crochet hook, 6 dc into an adjustable ring (6 sts).
Round 2: (2 dc into next st, 2 dc) twice (8 sts).
Round 3: (1 dc, 2 dc into next st) four times (12 sts).
Round 4: (2 dc, 2 dc into next st) four times (16 sts).
Round 5: (3 dc, 2 dc into next st) four times (20 sts).
Round 6: (4 dc, 2 dc into next st) four times (24 sts).
Round 7: 2 dc, 2 dc into next st, (5 dc, 2 dc into next st) three times, 3 dc (28 sts).
Round 8: (6 dc, 2 dc into next st) four times (32 sts).
Round 9: 3 dc, 2 dc into next st, (7 dc, 2 dc into next st) three times, 4 dc (36 sts).
Round 10: (8 dc, 2 dc into next st) four times (40 sts).
Fold the wing flat and line up the stitches on both sides of the opening. Work 1 dc in each pair of sts opposite each other along the top to close (20 sts).
Cut yarn, leaving a long enough tail for making up (**9**).

7

8

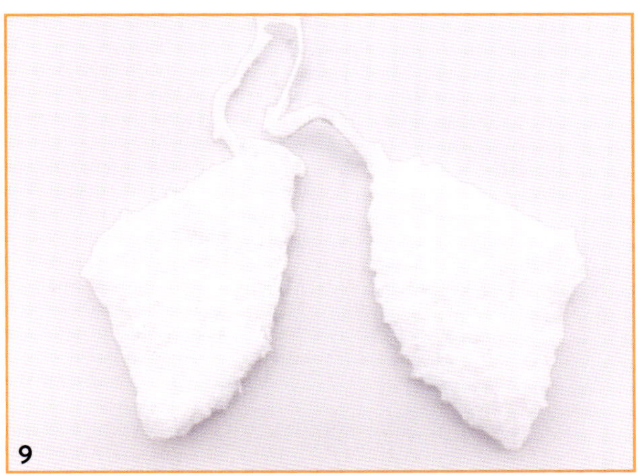
9

HEAD

Round 1: using yarn A, 8 dc into an adjustable ring (8 sts).
Round 2: (2 dc into next st) eight times (16 sts).
Round 3: (1 dc, 2 dc into next st) eight times (24 sts).
Round 4: (2 dc, 2 dc into next st) eight times (32 sts).
Round 5: (3 dc, 2 dc into next st) eight times (40 sts).
Round 6: 1 dc into each st around (40 sts).
Round 7: (4 dc, 2 dc into next st) eight times (48 sts).
Rounds 8–11 (4 rounds): 1 dc into each st around (48 sts).
Round 12: 24 dc, (dc2tog, 4 dc) four times (44 sts).
Rounds 13–15 (3 rounds): 1 dc into each st around (44 sts).
Round 16: 21 dc, (2 dc into next st, 2 dc) three times, 5 dc, (2 dc into next st, 2 dc) three times (50 sts).
Rounds 17–20 (4 rounds): 1 dc into each st around (50 sts).
Start stuffing the head, then continue stuffing as you go.
Round 21: (8 dc, dc2tog) five times (45 sts).
Round 22: 3 dc, dc2tog, (7 dc, dc2tog) four times, 4 dc (40 sts).
Round 23: (6 dc, dc2tog) five times (35 sts).
Round 24: 2 dc, dc2tog, (5 dc, dc2tog) four times, 3 dc (30 sts).
Round 25: (3 dc, dc2tog) six times (24 sts).
Round 26: 1 dc, dc2tog, (2 dc, dc2tog) five times, 1 dc (18 sts).
Cut yarn, leaving a long enough tail for making up.
Using yarn A, embroider a nose over sts 35 and 36 of round 16.
Using black embroidery thread, embroider eyes on either side of the nose on round 15, each 4 sts wide, and 4 sts apart (**4**).
Using brown embroidery thread, embroider eyebrows 3 rounds above each eye.
Apply pink blusher to the cheeks (**10**).

10

EAR (make 2)

Using yarn A, work 2 ch, 4 tr, 2 ch, 1 sl st into an adjustable ring. Pull to close ring.
Cut yarn, leaving a long enough tail for making up (**11**).

11

MAKING UP

Sew on the arms one round below the neck (**12**).

Sew the wings to the angel's back (**13**).

Pin the ears in place on either side of the head over rounds 14 and 16, approximately 4 sts from the eyes, then sew on (**14**).

Attach the head, adding a little more stuffing just before closing up (**15**).

Cut 12 lengths of yarn D, approximately 25cm (10in) each (**16**). Place them on the head, pinning the first strand into position (**17**). Using white embroidery thread, sew on the first strand, then the others one by one, using back stitch (**18, 19, 20 and 21**). Using your fingers, separate the fibres of each strand to give it some volume (**22**). Distribute the hair around the head, then sew it securely into place (**23**).

12

15

18

13

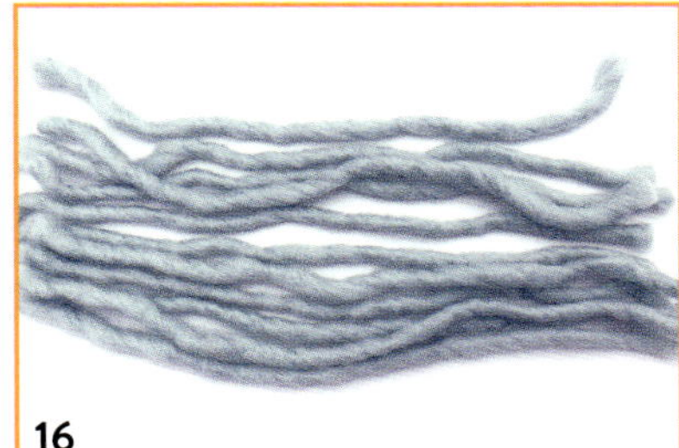

16

19

14

17

20

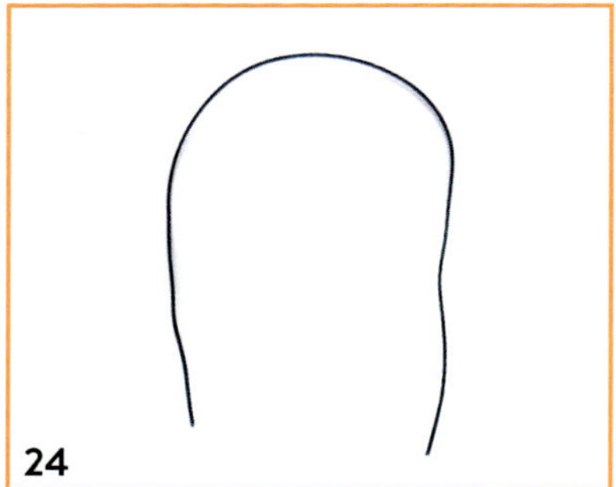

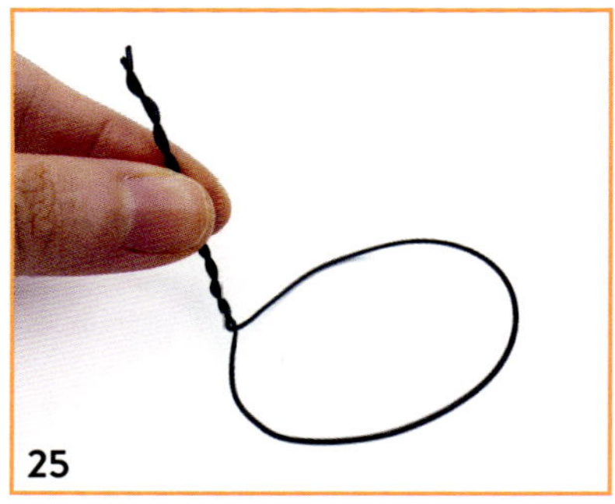

HALO (optional: for decoration only, not suitable for children)

Use a length of wire to form a ring, then twist the two ends around each other (**24 and 25**).

Using yarn F, work in dc around the wire to cover it (**26 and 27**). Cut yarn.

Place the halo on the angel's head, inserting the end into her hair; secure it using a few stitches to sew it in place (**28**).

Acknowledgements

Thank you to my little Anna who gives me the opportunity to enjoy Christmas through her excited eyes every year, and who has given me so much help and encouragement in choosing the characters in this book and deciding what to call them.

Thank you to my husband, Baptiste, who always helps me with the writing of my books and more broadly, provides me with the means to devote myself to crochet (and thanks to Santa Claus for having caused our paths to cross ten years ago).

Thank you to the whole team at Éditions Eyrolles for the trust they have placed in me once again, and for their professionalism. In particular, many thanks to Anne-Lise who suggested this new Christmas-themed project and who has been a brilliant companion while I was working on it.

Thank you to DMC France for their continued support, and particularly Assia for the care she has taken in helping me select the yarn.

Finally, I can never thank all you crocheters out there enough – without you I could never have turned my passion into my profession. I hope that we will continue on our way together for many years to come.

A thousand thanks!